TRUST CHILDREN

NATURAL LEARNING
FOR TWENTY-FIRST-CENTURY STUDENTS

"In this intelligent, insightful and deeply felt book, veteran teacher
Anne Cummings Jacopetti sheds light on the breathtaking
capacity for learning that all children possess. Jacopetti shares the
wisdom of fifty years on the front lines of learning in language
that is both straightforward and poetic, weaving together the
stories of individual children with her own astute analysis of how
learning really works. Jacopetti gives us ample evidence that the
totalizing, quantitative data-driven trends in American education
are not only wrongheaded — but antithetical to the natural
process of learning — indeed, to the development of intellect
itself. Jacopetti demonstrates in this slender, powerful book, that
learning is experiential, experimental, and qualitative in nature,
and that we would do well — as educators, parents, policy makers,
and citizens — to rethink the way we help children learn."
>> — **Marya Hornbacher,** best-selling author, Houghton Mifflin

"A beautiful book thoughtfully crafted. I enjoyed the studies you
chose to highlight. I did not read any errors of neuroscientific
discovery. thank you for contributing to the field in this way.
XOX"
>> — **Dr. Reggie Melrose,** stress and trauma specialist
>> and best-selling author of *The Sixty Seconds Fix*

"*Trust Children* provides tools for teachers to understand the
transformational task teaching really is — being an observer of
children, seeing each one, as well as the collective class, in a
process of growth and development. The teacher fosters this
development through carefully crafted encounters with the
world — through story, play, art, nature, conversation, etc. Anne
Jacopetti has essentialized what's needed, and educators and
educational settings of all kinds would benefit from studying
these universal concepts. Truly, the way forward is through
honoring the needs of children!"
>> — **Kalen Wood,** experienced Waldorf teacher
>> and administrator of Summerfield Waldorf School

TRUST CHILDREN

NATURAL LEARNING
FOR TWENTY-FIRST-CENTURY STUDENTS

ANNE CUMMINGS JACOPETTI

SANTA ROSA, CALIFORNIA

Better Learning Press
Santa Rosa, California 95403
howchildrenlearn.org

Publisher's Note: This is a revised edition of *What Are We Going To Learn Today?*, originally published in 2016. In addition to the new title, there is significant new content.

Ordering Information: Quantity sales. Special discounts are available on quantity purchases by corporations, associations, and others. For details, contact the publisher via the Contact Me page at the above website.

Cover design and text pages formatting by Lorna Johnson, lornajohnson.com
Project management by Ruth Schwartz, thewonderlady.com

Publisher's Cataloging-in-Publication data

Names: Jacopetti, Anne Cummings, author.

Title: Trust children : natural learning for twenty-first-century students / Anne Cummings Jacopetti.

Description: Santa Rosa, California : Better Learning Press, [2024] | "This is a revised edition of 'What Are We Going To Learn Today?', originally published in 2016. In addition to the new title, there is significant new content."--Title page verso. | Includes bibliographical references.

Indentifiers: ISBN: 979-8-9904784-0-4 (paperback) | 979-8-9904784-1-1 (ebook) | LCCN: 2024908910

Subjects: LCSH: Education--Aims and objectives. | Education--Philosophy. | Learning--Philosophy. | Learning ability--Study and teaching. | Teaching--Philosophy. | Learning, Psychology of. | Educational psychology. | Teaching--Handbooks, manuals, etc. | Child development. | BISAC: EDUCATION / Aims and Objectives. | EDUCATION / Learning Styles. | EDUCATION / Teaching / Methods & Strategies.

Classification: LCC: LB1025.3 .J33 2024 | DDC: 371.102--dc23

All I am saying in this book can be summed up
in two words — *Trust Children*.

Nothing could be more simple — or more difficult.

Difficult, because to trust children we must trust ourselves —
and most of us were taught as children
that we could not be trusted.

— John Holt, author of *How Children Learn*

Foreword

I just finished reading *Trust Children: Natural Learning for Twenty-First-Century Students* by Anne Cummings Jacopetti. Get a copy; read it; pass it on to teachers, parents, students, community members, and anyone interested in what schools and classrooms could be (and should be) at their best, as well as the challenges we face as we continue the struggle to create meaningful educational experiences for all children and youth.

This book is an illuminating read, filled with hard-won wisdom from a lifetime of teaching. Jacopetti writes beautifully, and her stories are packed with wisdom about the power of dialogue and questioning, curiosity, and first-hand experiences in teaching and authentic learning. She urges us to release our wildest imaginations as we nurture a tolerance for improvisation, confusion, experimentation, perpetual uncertainty, reciprocity, spontaneity, uniqueness, and flux.

And she helps us understand the terms of resistance. Education for free people is powered, after all, by a particularly precious and fragile ideal: Every human being is of infinite and incalculable value, each a work in progress and a force in motion, each a unique intellectual, emotional, physical, spiritual, moral, and creative force, each born equal in dignity and rights, each endowed with reason and conscience and agency, each deserving recognition and respect, and a dedicated place in a community of solidarity. We resist anything that dehumanizes or thingifies human beings, all the mechanisms to indoctrinate, inspect, rank, appraise, censure, order about, register, sort, admonish, and sermonize. And we recognize, further, that the fullest development of each individual — given the tremendous range of ability and the delicious stew of race, ethnicity, points of origin, and background — is the necessary condition for the full development of the entire community, and, conversely, that the fullest development of all is essential for the full development of each.

Jacopetti gets it: Learning is an entirely natural human pursuit, and we are learning all the time. Curiosity is inherent — living in a wildly complex and diverse human community is all the motivation we need to keep growing and learning.

Wherever and whenever questioning, researching, reimagining, rebuilding, pursuing authentic questions and interests and experiences, and undertaking active work in the community is the order of the day, a spirit of open communication, interchange, and analysis becomes commonplace as an expression of love. In these places there is a certain natural disorder, some anarchy and chaos, as there is in any busy workshop. But there is also a sense of joy, and a deeper discipline at work, the discipline of getting things done and learning with one another and through life. We see clearly in these cases that education at its best is always generative, for teachers and students alike.

—**Bill Ayres,** social justice activist, teacher,
distinguished professor of education (retired)
at the University of Illinois at Chicago;
author of two memoirs and *Demand the Impossible;*
creator of the podcast, *Under the Tree: a Seminar on Freedom*

Contents

Dedication

For all the children I have known
and in loving memory of
Alex Teal, Colin Postel,
Solomon Kahn, and Rory Harlib.

Introduction

What is the world made up of? This question lights up the first day of first grades in Waldorf schools all over the world. I introduced it to my class by telling the children a story about seven-year-old twins, Jarod and Jana, who were exploring the woods near their farmhouse.

Jarod and Jana smelled wildflowers, picked berries, and listened to the birds before they came upon an old man with a long gray beard and a kind smile sitting with his back against a large oak tree. He spoke to them by name, and they recognized him as a neighbor.

He said, "I have a question for you to take on your walk today. I will sit here and enjoy the birds with Grandmother Oak until you come back and show me what you have learned. My question for you is: what is the world made up of?"

Jarod and Jana were surprised and became even more aware of everything around them. They walked through the woods, looking high and low, seeking the answer to the old man's question.

At this point, I paused the story for a while, and the children went outside to look around and think about the question. When they came back, I asked them what they had discovered, and they put their gleanings on the Nature Table.

When Jarod and Jana came back to Grandmother Oak, the old man was dozing. They sat quietly at his feet until he woke up. "Tell me, tell me, what have you found?" he asked.

Jarod took a twig, a long blade of grass, and the stalk of a cattail out of his backpack and said, "I think that the world is made up of straight lines." The old man nodded and smiled. Then he asked Jana what she had discovered.

Jana reached into her jacket pocket and brought out a flower, an oak leaf, some choke cherries, and a small, rounded stone. She said, "I think that the world is made up of curves."

And the old man said, "You are both right! Yes, the world is made up of straight lines and curves."

My first-graders looked around the room to find examples of straight lines and curves while I passed out drawing paper and their first set of block crayons, rolled up in corduroy bags, one for each child. When we finished talking about what they had noticed, they began their first drawings — a straight line and a curve — shapes that would be the foundation for all of the drawings and letters they would make in the days to come.

The story did not end there. Jarod and Jana rejoined the class often, bringing their lives on the farm to our math lessons. The children and I had shared an experience that allowed us to see the world around us in a new way as we embarked together on a years-long journey of discovery.

Some years after my first graders had graduated from high school, I received a phone call from Israel from a former member of this class. She said, "Ms. C., I have to tell you what just happened!" She told me about a workshop led by a famous ballerina, who began by asking the dance students what they thought that dance was made up of. Hannah said that she waved her hand and told everyone, "Dance is made up of straight lines and curves!" and the surprised teacher said, "Exactly. You are right!"

Yesterday, I asked my teenage grandsons, who attended a Waldorf charter school, what the world is made up of, and they responded immediately with "Straight lines and curves!" (Actually, the younger one said "Cheese!" first and then grinned and gave me the right answer.)

This iconic first-grade lesson has been successful over the decades because it respects children and the ways they learn. It asks a big question at just the right moment. I remember a son at this age asking me as I tucked him into bed, "Why are we here, Mom? What is this all about?" Children also like to look for answers. They love to explore and find things. They like to play with and use what they have learned to make it their own. They all love to listen to stories.

I began my inquiry for *Trust Children* by identifying activities that immediately engage students of all ages, and I soon realized that there is a direct connection between the natural ways that children have learned throughout human history and the activities in school that they respond to with enthusiasm. This respect for natural learning that is foundational in Waldorf schools is, I believe, the primary reason that the Waldorf movement has grown over the last hundred years to become the largest independent school movement in the world, with over twelve hundred schools and two thousand kindergartens in seventy-five countries.[1]

Understanding of natural learning is evolving, deepened by break-throughs in brain science. We know now that newborns are not *tabula rasas,* blank slates just waiting for input from their environments. Recent experiments demonstrate that infants start learning language in the womb and can recognize specific sound patterns at birth.[2] We know that infants and young children are prodigious learners who amaze their parents and grandparents as they figure out how to move and coordinate their bodies, how to communicate with their families, and how to understand and function in the world around them. They are curious. They are resilient, and they respond enthusiastically to learning opportunities that recognize and respect their innate abilities, needs, and accomplishments. They make enormous strides without formal instruction, although it is also understood that the quality of their relationships and the conditions present in their environment have direct impacts on what they are able to accomplish.

Brain research informs us that children's brains are particularly neuroplastic and have double the number of neural connections present in adult brains.[3] Repeated actions preserve synapses that form new brain patterns. Every new experience stimulates the brain to rewire its physical structure. Synapses that are not activated are pruned and disappear. All children have potential abilities that may not be developed because they are not recognized or encouraged. How we parent and educate children profoundly influences their brain patterns, thus the kind of human beings they are able to become and, by extension, the kind of societies they are able to create. Please stop reading for a moment and take that in.

We also know that child development progresses through predictable stages as young brains mature and establish new patterns. We do not expect second-grade children to write expository essays. High school students do not usually spend their recesses playing hopscotch and jump rope. We know that individual development is also variable. Some children require more time than others to accomplish similar academic goals. Some children carry unusual gifts and capacities. Some have neurological or physical challenges. Each child is a complicated equation of inherited proclivities and environmental influences. No two children are the same.

What they do share, however, are generally positive responses to activities that human beings have developed through the millennia as learning tools for survival that their brains seem to be either prewired for or at least prepared to expect. These activities support the development of the five natural learning systems — emotional, social, cognitive, physical, and reflective — that neuroscientists identify as primary for full brain development.[4] When the needs of each of these interconnected systems are met, students develop into self-motivated, active learners capable of collaboration, strategic thinking, and purposeful reflection. Deprivation of or overreliance on a particular system may result in students who tend to be egocentric, unmotivated, overly analytic, self-doubting, or antisocial.[5] The natural learning activities described in each chapter of *Trust Children* work together to support the balanced development of children's brains. These activities engage "head, heart, and hands" and promote the interconnected development of thinking, feeling, and doing—an education of and for the whole child.

Play is a primary instinctual activity that children share with the animal kingdom, providing a safe space for learning new skills, trying out ideas, and meeting challenges. Learning to play together develops social skills, adaptability, intelligence, creativity, and more. Play is a driving force behind neurogenesis and has a significant role in sculpting children's brains, particularly their prefrontal lobes.

Stories have been primary teaching tools throughout human history. Preliterate cultures used stories to pass on information essential for survival and social cohesion. Stories help children begin to make sense of the world and give them compasses to navigate challenges in addition to developing their imaginations. Brain research suggests that our brains are particularly patterned to remember them.

The connection of playful activity to the arts is implicit in our language. We play instruments, we act in plays in which we play different characters, and we create objects, images, and stories that arc through time to connect us with past and future generations. The arts are essential to learning and developing creativity, self-confidence, problem solving, perseverance, focus, collaboration, and responsibility. They have been primary forms of personal and cultural expression throughout human history.

Asking questions and learning through doing interweave as children strive to understand their environment and develop capabilities for effective and thoughtful action. Experiences that provide possible answers to children's questions motivate them to become enthusiastic learners. The questions that don't have easy answers are the most powerful.

Throughout most of human history, we have lived in a close relationship with the natural world. Careful observation and management of resources are necessary to maintain a balance necessary for survival. Our current degree of separation from nature not only damages modern children but also threatens their survival. Mental development and physical health are impacted by the number of hours children spend staring at virtual worlds on screens instead of playing outside in sunlight, fresh air, and natural surroundings.

A bonded, attached relationship with at least one trusted adult is the most essential condition for learning. Infants and toddlers who are deprived of this relationship fail to thrive. Although primary attachment is usually with a parent, teachers can form strong secondary relationships with the children in their care. Relationship is the door to learning. If this door remains shut or only ajar, real learning will be limited.

When a teacher forms a trusting relationship with a group of children, they form a community that, over time, provides them with support, collaborative skills, and lasting friendships. Community meets a primary human need so intense that loneliness, which afflicts many modern individuals, has been recently characterized as a disease response to social isolation. Together, children learn how to talk, how to listen, how to think, and how to make decisions. The community that develops as the children mature prepares them for future engagement in civic life. Such classroom communities are strengthened through school-wide celebrations that recognize cultural heritage and offer opportunities to practice gratitude and appreciation for our bountiful planet and each other.

It follows that educational programs that respect and utilize attached relationships and natural learning proclivities and that adapt to meet children's developmental needs will be more successful at enthusiastically engaging children in the learning process than programs that do not recognize their importance. This seems obvious, but our current education system has persisted in cutting back or eliminating play time, story time, recess, field trips, the arts, and humanities so that children will have more time to study for tests with an emphasis on non-fiction, science, math, and facts—often introduced at an inappropriate age. In addition, rigid schedules and the arbitrary separation of subjects fundamentally ignore the importance of systemic relationships and community and routinely disrupt relationships among teachers and students.

Enough. Everyone can remember sitting too long in an uncomfortable chair, listening to a teacher's voice drone on. Any teacher who has attempted to teach grammar out of a textbook to a group of eighth graders knows what an exercise in futility feels like. Our outdated teach-to-the-test educational system is not able to realize its own objectives. Too many children are failing. Too many are being stressed and limited in their development. Too many are being divided into "winners" and "losers." This is no way to treat children, who are unarguably our most precious resource.

The time is overripe for change. The capacities and skills twenty-first-century students must develop to meet the multiple challenges presented by our changing climate have been identified by numerous authorities. A Brookings Institute study identifies critical thinking/reasoning, creativity/creative thinking, problem solving, metacognition, collaboration, communication, and global citizenship.[6] The authors conclude that current educational systems are not providing instruction that supports the development of these skills. Environmentalists stress the importance of systemic consciousness—the ability to identify the "patterns that connect" that enable us to understand and to be responsible for the systemic consequences of our actions down to the "seventh generation." Thom Markham, an international education consultant, identifies the development of empathy as the primary factor underlying the development of all these capacities.[7]

How must our established education systems be transformed so that all children can thrive and be better prepared to co-create a more sustainable and equitable world? "Transformed" is the key word. Sir Ken Robinson's *Creative Schools: The Grassroots Movement That Is Transforming Education* (2015) offers a strong critique of our current system and a hopeful survey of transformative educational initiatives he investigated across the United States and the United

Kingdom.[8] *Sustainability, Human Well-Being and the Future of Education,* published by Sitra, the Finnish Innovation Fund, offers eighteen inspiring descriptions of initiatives that are transforming educational opportunities for groups of students in Finland and the United States.[9] In many of these projects, siloed subjects are exchanged for systemic approaches that explore the connections between human beings, nature, cultures, and economies. Teachers in such schools are facilitators and coaches in cross-generational communities of inquiry and action centered on student-generated questions and concerns. Transdisciplinary studies lead to real-world engagement, where students learn that they can make a difference. The programs Sitra describes offer a new approach to learning, one that respects and trusts students and their natural proclivities and envisions school as a collaborative community committed to the ongoing transformation of self, school, and society. (See Epilogue for a more detailed summary of Sitra's initiatives.)

Trust Children also takes inspiration from Bill Ayres, education professor emeritus and lifelong activist, who writes in his manifesto *Demand the Impossible!*

> *Education for free people is powered by a particularly precious and fragile ideal. Every human being is of infinite and incalculable value, each a work in progress and a force in motion, each a unique intellectual, emotional, physical, spiritual, moral and creative force, each of us born equal in dignity and rights, each endowed with reason and conscience and agency, each deserving a dedicated place in a community of solidarity as well as a vital sense of brotherhood and sisterhood, recognition and respect. Embracing that basic ethic and spirit, people recognize that the fullest development of each individual — given the tremendous range of ability and the delicious stew of race, ethnicity, points of origin, and background — is the necessary condition for the full development of the entire community, and, conversely, that the fullest development of all is essential for the full development of each.[10]*

Trust Children describes how respecting and utilizing the natural ways children learn supports the development of each child while building a vibrant "community of solidarity." These activities and principles can be implemented in all subjects at all grade levels. They are effective for all children regardless of their places in the "delicious stew" of diversity because all children, regardless of their ethnicity, cultural background, or language development, share the same basic proclivities for natural learning.

Applying these basic principles stimulates a fundamental change in awareness in teachers as well as students, a change analogous to the current shift in the way we look at the soil in our farms and gardens. Instead of seeing growing beds as settings that require chemical amendments, fertilizers, pesticides, and treated seeds to ensure maximum growth, we are learning to foster regeneration by collaborating with the invisible web of interconnected microbial and plant life that teems under our feet. Instead of progressively destroying topsoil, we are learning how to support it to sequester the excess carbon in the atmosphere while we grow healthier food. In the same spirit, we can begin to look at each child as an infinitely valuable "force in motion," filled with surprises and inherent qualities that we can observe, support, and celebrate. We can encourage groups of children to bring their individual gifts to the questions and challenges that most engage them. Respecting the natural ways that children learn is the beginning of a collaborative journey for children and teachers, a journey that will fundamentally transform our schools and help to educate motivated, skilled, and reflective young citizens primed to meet the unprecedented challenge of possible extinction by creating a more equitable, vibrant, and sustainable future for themselves and coming generations.

Chapter One

Voices from the Past

What was educationally significant and hard to measure has been replaced by what is educationally insignificant and easy to measure. So now we measure how well we taught what isn't worth learning.
— **Arthur Costa**, emeritus education professor,
Cal State University, Sacramento

Thirty-eight sophomores were taking turns reading *Julius Caesar* out loud. The student playing Caesar was near the end of his final speech in Act III, Scene 2 when the door burst open. A student stuck his head in and shouted, "The president has been shot! The president has been shot!"

After a long moment of silence, Caesar read, "Et tu Brute?" and we closed our books. It was late morning, November 23, 1963. I was in the second month of the decades-long arc of my teaching career.

Kennedy's assassination brought a tragic end to a year that had seen the struggle for civil rights and racial equality erupt in Birmingham and across the South. Martin Luther King inspired us with his "I Have a Dream" speech at the Lincoln Memorial. Against the looming threat of war in Viet Nam, the first nuclear test ban treaty was signed with Russia, putting a temporary halt to a terrifying arms race that had teetered on the brink of a nuclear exchange in 1961. Change was in the air. Betty Friedan published *The Feminine Mystique,* and the Beatles appeared on *The Ed Sullivan*

Show. How was I going to bridge these contemporary events and my school's conservative standard English curriculum as 150 students, in classes tracked as Y+, Y, and Y-, came through my classroom each day? My question was poised to become a national conversation.

John Holt's passionate indictments of our educational system, *How Children Fail* and *How Children Learn*, were published in 1964. *How Children Fail* contains a diary of Holt's observations of his middle school students, their struggles with math, and the strategies they used to hide their confusion. He concluded that school had damaged their intellectual and creative capacities by transforming their natural self-confidence into fear of failure. Blocked from developing their own interests and capacities and encouraged instead to work for petty rewards — gold stars, A's, and honor rolls — his students had been trained by age ten to repeat what they had been told whether they understood it or not. Their days and evenings were filled with dull, repetitive tasks as they struggled to remember arbitrary and disconnected hunks of information that were often irrelevant to their lives. In the process, his students were being trained to become unintelligent adults, unable to think clearly or respond appropriately to life's challenges. The children who failed to meet standards learned that they were stupid and stopped trying. The "good" students learned that they were smart and better than others because they could consistently reproduce "right" answers, a process that stifled their curiosity and creativity.[11]

Holt called on educators to stop traumatizing children and to transform schools into places that trust and respect children's natural capacities. *How Children Learn* supports this vision with careful observation and analysis of how preschool children learn to talk, read, count, and reason.

> *The child is curious. He wants to make sense out of things, find out how things work, gain competence and control over himself and his environment, do what he can see other people doing. He is open, receptive and perceptive. He does not shut himself off from the strange, confused, complicated world around him.*

He observes it closely and sharply, tries to take it all in. He is experimental. He does not merely observe the world around him, but tastes it, touches it, hefts it, bends it, breaks it... He is not afraid of making mistakes. And he is patient. He can tolerate an extraordinary amount of uncertainty, confusion, ignorance and suspense. He is willing and able to wait for meaning to come to him — even if it comes very slowly, which it usually does.[12]

Holt's books struck a resonant chord. They were translated into forty-one languages, sold millions of copies, and sparked many attempts at educational reform, including parent-run free schools and the home-schooling movement. His observations inspired intense conversations in my cadre of beginning teachers in UC Berkeley's Graduate Internship Program. Challenged by Holt's observations, we wanted to teach children without damaging them, and we began to observe our students carefully to understand how we could make their concerns and interests a more central focus in our classrooms. We hoped to build a more just society by inspiring students to ask questions, challenge authority, and deal with real issues, not only as they were reported in the daily newspapers and TV channels but also in the schools themselves and the daily lives of our students in their various neighborhoods and communities. These aspirations were in direct conflict with long-established pedagogical attitudes and norms and stimulated lively disputes among our faculties and administrations.

Students in my Y- English classes had accepted their categorization as "students who aren't going to excel in English." How to inspire them to overcome this labeling? I purchased a class set of *Black Like Me,* the story of a white man who described how his experience as an American changed when he artificially darkened his skin and was perceived as African American.[13] We read and discussed this book before I invited fellow intern Terry Borton, who was teaching in a nearby school where the majority of students were African American, to bring a group of his students to my all-white classes. We had an open discussion about race relations in the students' respective schools and communities, a first for most of them. Afterward, I introduced a five-paragraph essay format as a way for my students to effectively communicate what they had learned from the book and the encounter. They all turned in their first essays. Later that week, the principal summoned me and asked what I was doing talking about race in my classes instead of teaching English. I showed him the pile of essays. His response, after he looked them over, was that many of these students had been "mis-tracked," that they were too proficient in English to be in a Y- class. Exactly.

The following year, Terry received a grant to create an innovative summer program at the Friends' Select School in Philadelphia. Half of our applicants came from predominantly white private academies, and the other half from predominantly African American public schools. Our task was to develop a level playing field that would turn racial and cultural diversity into an educational asset. I decided to use Viola Spolin's improvisational drama exercises,[14] which require students to work together to create scenes and solve problems.

We began with simple exercises, like the Mirror Exercise, in which two students take turns initiating and mirroring each other's actions and expressions while maintaining eye contact. From a somewhat tense beginning, the students quickly created a shared safe space. I was amazed by their courage and willingness to take risks as they reached across deep cultural barriers to make contact. I remember one improvisation done with the students behind a raised curtain with only their feet visible. A pair of large black feet and a pair of small white feet approached each other and then stopped, obviously unsure about how to proceed. A foot conversation followed that changed from fear and mistrust to interest as the feet moved closer and closer. Finally, after several false starts, the feet touched. Tenderly, the large black foot reached out and stroked the small white foot, which responded in turn. The scene ended with a foot hug. Some of the students in the audience had tears in their eyes as we clapped. I know I did. We did not talk about this, however. We talked about the process and whether the scene solved the problem well. We laughed a lot that summer and sometimes cried, and the six weeks were over much too soon. We had successfully realized the objectives of our project, but we also had to face that our students were experiencing grief at the abrupt end of their new relationships with us and each other.

I received a grant several years later to introduce a similar year-long improvisational drama program in two Berkeley junior high schools that had recently been integrated. Again, I watched diverse groups of students appreciate the opportunity to co-create and learn to improvise together. I observed they were also becoming friends. One of the administrators asked how I was going to assess whether the program had worked. He described my goals as somewhat nebulous and said he wanted quantitative results. I was pondering how to do this when another tragic event gave the strongest possible qualitative answer to his question. Martin Luther King was assassinated in Memphis on April 4, 1968. The next day, the African American students at the junior high school named for him walked out — except for one class. The students in the improvisational drama program came to class, put their arms around each other, wept, and found consolation through their shared grief and dismay.

Terry described these projects and others that followed in *Reach, Touch and Teach,* published in 1970. My co-teacher from the Philadelphia project, Peter Kleinbard, had invited me to join a summer program at Berkeley High School that reaffirmed what can happen when students are given agency and allowed to collaborate with teachers. Terry described this program in his book and recorded the following student observations:

> *I feel more spongy, like I have a new interest in things: ballet, opera, art galleries, 15 million wonderful ways — there's a door opening somewhere in me, I can feel the key in the lock.*
>
> *Right now, I feel daring, unafraid to do what I can towards being the person I'm capable of being. Less afraid to fail to be that person.* [15]

Berkeley's Community High School Summer Program was an early model for the movement to establish small independent programs within large schools, an idea that has spread widely during the past several decades.

On the national front, however, educational reforms subsided with the seventies. John Holt published a second edition of *How Children Learn* in 1983.

> *Since I wrote this book our schools have with few exceptions moved steadily and often rapidly in the wrong direction. Schools are on the whole bigger than they used to be, more depersonalized, more threatening, more dangerous… Teachers have even less to say than they used to about what they teach and how they teach and test it. The schools cling more and more stubbornly to the mistaken idea that education and teaching are industrial processes, to be designed and planned from above in the minutest detail and then imposed on passive teachers and their even more passive students.*[16]

In 1983, the Reagan administration decided to promote "Back to Basics," a movement focused on math, science, and English, created in the late 1970s by conservatives who were threatened by progressive change and wanted to bar social issues like civil rights and black history from school curricula. The National Commission of Excellence in Education, formed by William Bennett, Ronald Reagan's Secretary of Education, published *A Nation at Risk* — an alarm bell that cited American students' mediocre performance on international tests as a major threat to national security. "Our schools are failing" became the mantra for decades of school reform. Back to Basics later morphed into No Child Left Behind during the Bush administration and Race to the Top under Obama. These programs spent billions of dollars to improve performance on tests measuring basic skills in math, English, and science. Poor test results were used to withdraw federal funding from failing schools and to justify privatization — transferring government funding from locally controlled public schools to for-profit charter schools. All of these initiatives failed to significantly improve overall student test performance.[17] There is, unfortunately, no way to measure the harm they have done and are doing to children, teachers, and schools in the process.

I was horrified by Back to Basics and its emphasis on rote learning. I did not want to be straitjacketed by school district policies that marginalized the arts and strictly controlled subject content. I was particularly alarmed by a policy in some of our local schools that required teachers at the same level to be on the same page of a scripted textbook on the same day, using the same words, and administering the same test to their classes. Trusting children and their interests was not an option in such a scenario. And such programs certainly did not trust me. I felt increasingly that I was not only unable to accomplish my goals and aspirations for my students but also that I was doing them serious harm by going through the required paces.

On one such afternoon, when the bell rang just as we were reaching the cusp of an important discussion and my students rushed out the door to their next subject, I found myself slipping down and sitting, curled up, in the well of my desk. Before I could collect myself, I heard footsteps and my next class coming in for the last period. Minutes passed as I considered how I would explain why I was sitting under my desk. I finally took a deep breath and crawled out, only to discover that my students were sitting quietly under their desks, waiting for me. That day, we pushed our desks back, sat in a circle on the floor, and talked about school and life. I bet they remember it, too. It was time for me to make a change.

My friend and mentor, Mary Caroline Richards, had recently published *Toward Wholeness: Rudolf Steiner Education in America*.[18] I was particularly struck by what M.C. called "a grammar of interconnections" in a pedagogy that connected scientific observation, artistic imagination, and practical activity, with each part bearing a deep connection to the whole. I was also impressed that Waldorf teachers were encouraged to use artistic activities in all subjects and instruction was structured to respect children's developmental ages. A visit to a peaceful, beautiful Waldorf kindergarten, filled with children who were busy playing and helping to prepare lunch, warmed my heart. I handed in my resignation at the public school where I was teaching, took a leap of faith, and gratefully accepted a job teaching fourth grade at Marin Waldorf School.

For the next quarter-century, Waldorf schools were my learning ground. I studied at Rudolf Steiner College in Fair Oaks, California, each summer and later joined a training class at Summerfield Waldorf School designed for teachers who were already experienced in the classroom. I helped to pioneer a Waldorf high school in Santa Rosa and, after eight years, returned to Marin to teach a large, ebullient group of children as they progressed from first through eighth grade. Before full retirement, I worked as a school mentor and then as educational director for two Waldorf-inspired public charter schools.

Rudolph Steiner (1861–1925) was an Austrian philosopher, scientist, artist, and clairvoyant whose career and creative initiatives defy conventional categories. He designed the first Waldorf school, which opened in Stuttgart, Germany, in 1919 as an alternative to the rigidly tracked Austrian educational system. A century later, Steiner's vision has developed into the largest independent school movement in the world. The last decade has also produced a growing number of Waldorf-inspired public charter schools.

Like John Holt, Rudolf Steiner developed his pedagogy by carefully observing children at different stages of development. In a 1906 treatise on education, he wrote, "The essence of the developing child itself will reveal the appropriate educational guidelines." The guidelines for the first Waldorf school respect individual differences among children and focus on building neurological strength and integration through physical/sensory and emotional learning before stressing academics. The core curriculum, which is presented in two-hour main lessons for three- or four-week blocks, is designed to support and mirror children's developmental stages. Within this structure, teachers are free to shape instruction to the needs of the children in their classes and are encouraged to use their creative talents to bring the curriculum alive. Children access learning about history, mathematics, literature, and science through lessons that incorporate art, music, movement, speech, reading, storytelling, hands-on experimentation, practical life skills, and connection to nature. Subjects come and go, but long-term relationships between teachers and students are considered essential. Teachers in the elementary school specialize in teaching a particular group of children rather than subjects or grades, and they share the learning curve with their students as they explore new subjects, ideas, and activities during their eight-year collaboration.

Steiner envisioned schools that would provide safe and stimulating environments for children and teachers to develop their innate capacities. He designed an education for the whole child — head, heart, and hands — that he believed would protect children from becoming cogs in an impersonal machine of material fabrication and consumption. Instead, their education would support them to become free human beings, able to think for themselves, with the courage to act intelligently, creatively, and compassionately within their communities.[19] This is a tall order, but even striving to realize this vision builds character in teachers as well as students.

Waldorf schools struggle between two forces — the imperative to protect the dynamic vision Steiner launched with the first Waldorf school and the dogmatism that can grow over time that repeats gestures without questioning their purpose. My struggle between these forces, trying to understand the first and resist the second, lasted for all of my years as a Waldorf teacher. What I learned in the process was invaluable. Steiner wanted his Waldorf school to be a pilot program for the education of all children, an education that continually connects our human past to the future carried within the children. Trusting children, in this context, means embracing continual change and transformation within a structure that protects children from forces that would stifle their curiosity, natural creativity, and capacities for empathy and social responsibility — all qualities that we desperately need to support if we hope to resolve our current ecological and social crises.

John Holt and Rudolf Steiner were the primary voices from the past that entered the present with me each day as I opened the door of my classroom and greeted the children. Their voices guided my preparations and responses to the children once the day had begun. Their support gave me the courage to embark on a process of continual growth. I had to learn to trust myself to become a model for my students. I had to develop humility for the limit of my knowledge based on past experience and a deep appreciation for the unknown challenges of a future that would be created by the children, knowing that the way that I met them in the present moment would affect the way that they and the future that they carry are able to develop.

The children that my readers will meet in the coming chapters have grown into creative, thoughtful, and responsible adults, but the principles of natural learning that we gleaned from our shared experience have not changed. The world has changed in many ways over the years. My grandchildren have different brains than I, already adapted to this world of instant information and imagery that frequently befuddles my aging brain. They help me with my computer and encourage me to make friends with my Android phone. But the ways that they learn best are the same ways that their parents and I learned. The underlying principles of natural learning have not changed. These enduring practices hold the keys to our full development and to our ability to meet the challenges of change.

Chapter Two

Relationship Is the Crucible for Learning

My hero is someone who wakes up every morning and loves the world all over again.

—Hannah, age fourteen

I am surprised that I can remember so little about some of my teachers. I can't recall what they looked like, their names, or a single thing I learned from them. I must have turned in assignments and taken in enough to pass tests, but I have retained nothing about them in my long-term memory.

On the other hand, I will never forget my ninth-grade English teacher, Sophie Ryan, who inspired us with her passion for poetry and made us laugh and sometimes cheer and applaud. Or Stanley Cavell, UC Berkeley philosophy of religion professor, who taught us about the metaphorical nature of language. Or Bob Goldsby, who opened the doors to the world of theater. These teachers touched and inspired me. They helped me know myself and begin to find my place in the world.

Relationship is the crucible for learning. Teachers who present lessons without first connecting with their students are serving their soup on a plate instead of a bowl. All the ingredients may be there, but there is nothing to hold them, so they don't get taken in and digested. Children who have not been gathered up tend to become bored and restless and may begin to act out. Teachers often become frustrated and punitive in response, and learning is canceled for the day. Unfortunately, this can be the scenario day after day after day.

A teacher who trusts children and understands how to connect with them may bring a well-prepared lesson to class. But this teacher focuses first on the children: He wants to know what they know about the subject and asks them questions. He listens carefully and adapts what he presents to include their questions and observations. He lets the students know by the way that he listens to them that he respects them and wants to hear what they think. He gives this process all the time it needs and does not cut it short to fit a predetermined schedule. He doesn't start to present the lesson until all students are engaged.

A trusting relationship develops when a teacher consistently brings this attention to the children in his class. Disciplinary problems disappear, and multidimensional learning begins. The teacher models and encourages curiosity and awareness of multiple perspectives and possibilities. Students copy their teacher's behavior and learn to listen with interest to each other. Learning becomes dynamic as students articulate and begin to explore the questions emerging from their shared consciousness. The process I am describing is basic at all levels, first grade through college, and applies to all students.

This primary importance of relationship to learning begins at birth and extends through childhood and beyond. Attachment theory demonstrates how profoundly the quality of our early relationships is connected to healthy physical, emotional, and mental development.[20] Parents provide the safe haven that children require as they begin to explore the world. They also provide the models that show children how to survive the challenges the world presents. Children who do not experience secure and dependable relationships with their parents are at severe risk. Every aspect of their emotional, physical, and mental growth is affected negatively.

This is the tragedy that unfolds inexorably when children are separated from their parents at borders or through incarceration, illness, death, or other crises in their parents' lives.

Psychologists deem this basic attachment relationship indispensable to teaching as well as parenting. In *Hold On to Your Kids*, Gordon Neufeld and Gabor Maté connect the breakdown of strong attachment relationships to a rise in youth crime, bullying, drug use, suicide, and violence.[21]

Neufeld and Maté demonstrate that children can't endure an attachment void. They will look to their peers if they are not firmly attached to adults. Such children become increasingly detached from family life and school. They do not easily give us their attention, respect, or cooperation, yet they lack the experience and brain development to make good decisions on their own or provide trustworthy support for each other.

Parents and school authorities activate counterwill in such students when they react punitively to force compliance with rules or zero-tolerance policies. Ultimately, no one wins. Such peer-attached children too frequently move through suspensions to expulsions and into the prison system. Tragically, the primary goal of education — to guide children's development so they realize their potential and eventually make positive contributions to society — is lost.

Behavior modification systems, based on rewards and punishments, stifle healthy development. Neufeld directs us instead to see children's behavior as communication and to observe their behavior to uncover where they are stuck, whether through trauma, developmental challenges, or anxiety. The first step is to ensure that a child feels safe by gathering her up with consistent authority. (*I see you. I am here for you. Together, we can do this.*) A safe child can begin to relax, allow herself to become vulnerable, and finally come to "tears of futility" about what has happened to her and what can't be changed. This process builds the resilience children need for healthy, adaptive growth.[22]

This is easier said than done.

There are no set formulas for making a strong connection with a child, particularly one who is acting out of distress. Dr. Neufeld describes this process as "walking the maze." A parent or teacher who enters the maze to reconnect with a struggling child may encounter multiple dead ends before trust is established. The child must trust and become attached to the adult before they can be led out of the maze. This process may have to happen repeatedly before healthy growth is restored.

When parents and extended families are in crisis, a teacher may provide a child's only safety net. Far more than academic learning is at stake. The good news is that research confirms what experience has affirmed, that an attached and trusting relationship in which the caregiver perceives the child's needs accurately and responds consistently in a timely manner actually creates biochemical changes that can heal trauma, ease anxiety, and restore healthy growth.[23]

Students First, an online advocacy group, held a six-word essay contest on the topic "What makes a great teacher?" One of the winning responses (out of twenty-eight thousand submissions) spoke to the importance of relationship and attachment to learning: "I struggled. She never gave up." The story behind these words describes what it means to see and believe in a student's potential and, above all, not to wobble in that belief. A teacher (or parent) who remains unconditionally committed despite resistance and failures builds a relationship built on trust rather than threats and bribes.

I was not aware of attachment theory through most of my teaching career, but I learned quickly how important it was to make a strong, trusting relationship with each class of students. Trying to teach without that bond can be a miserable and futile way to spend an hour. Students who are not yet firmly connected can present challenges to patience, classroom management, and mood. How teachers respond to such challenges makes a big difference in outcomes for the whole group.

Jasper entered our class in fourth grade. His distress at having to change schools and be in a group of unknown children was palpable. He concentrated his upset in an unblinking glare that he spent most of class time directing toward me during our first weeks together. Jasper was obviously bright and capable but declined to work. He was, however, willing to participate in artistic activities. He ignored my suggestions during his first attempt at a watercolor painting exercise and ended up with a brown mess on his paper. I looked at his painting and made the mistake of trying to reassure him. Jasper picked up the painting and rubbed it down his face and the front of his white shirt, saying loudly, "I'm going to kill myself!"

There was a moment of shocked silence in the classroom. Then I smiled at him and said, "OK, but maybe we should wash your face first." He looked up at me with a glimmer of a smile behind his scowl and followed me to the sink. Our relationship had begun.

What happened in this exchange that made it pivotal? Perhaps a better question is what *could* have happened. I could have become alarmed and reported Jasper to the administration as suicidal. I could have scolded him for making a mess of himself and his desk. I could have sent him outside of the classroom. I could have called his mother to voice my concerns. The possibilities are many. Instead, I responded intuitively. Behind my words was an attitude that said, "I see how you feel. I can handle this. We are going to get through this together." I remember this moment because it was an "aha" moment for me as a teacher. The tension in the room dissolved; and the other children relaxed. I walked over to the sink. Jasper followed me, and I helped him wash his face. He allowed me to touch him for the first time. This moment was the door to a years-long relationship that would be challenging but full of growth for us both.

When I reacted to students out of my own conditioning and allowed my emotional buttons to be pushed, I could not be present in the moment. When I fell back on a system of consequences or rules, I did not give my intuition a chance. Each school day is filled with such existential choices that determine the quality of relationship between students and teacher and the amount of trust that is built or lost.

It is easy to miss these moments during the bustle of a normal school day. A good practice for teachers (or parents) is to take time before sleeping to review the day that has passed, to sit or lie quietly at bedtime with eyes closed and rerun the interactions of the day. Missed opportunities, responses that shut down relationship and learning rather than opening them up, have a way of popping into consciousness. When I was able to recognize and take responsibility for these inevitable lapses, I could make amends and rebuild trust the next day.

Sometimes, we don't even suspect that we have missed the boat and are saved only by keeping our eyes open. I remember a boy I taught briefly during the experimental summer project in Philadelphia. I went downstairs to the lunchroom after our drama class and saw him sitting alone and looking very sad. I knew that his life at home was extremely challenging. He was usually quiet, withdrawn deeply into himself. I sat down next to him and said, "You look sad. Has something happened? Can I help?"

He didn't speak for a few moments and then looked at me with tears in his eyes and said, "You know, Anne, when you stood at the door at the end of class?" I nodded. "Well, you touched everyone who passed by you, but you didn't touch me."

There was nothing to do in that moment except to say, "Oh, Chris, I'm so sorry." He let me give him a hug. Our project was over a few days later, but that moment is still with me. When I started to write about this memory, I thought that it was an example of following through, of noticing and responding. I realize now, as I write these words, that it has stayed with me all of these years because of a failure on my part. A door opened that day. I was face to face with Chris in the maze. He had allowed himself to become incredibly vulnerable, but I didn't take him by the hand. I didn't stay in touch with him when the project ended. He was reaching out for something far more than the hug I gave him.

Teaching children is an awesome responsibility. I had a mentor who laughingly described it as a spiritual fast track. There is no way to be fully equal to the task. Trying to be good at what I am describing works no better than trying to be enlightened. Children do not want us to try to be their friends or to try to make them like us. Bribes, threats, and treats, which are commonly used, do not work. Children need us to be caring adults they can respect as role models and trust to hold clear boundaries. But we must hold our alpha role of responsibility and leadership with humility and deep respect and love for the young human beings in our charge. A good sense of humor helps enormously, that and the fact that children are very forgiving.

Otto Scharmer, in *The Essentials of Theory U: Core Principles and Applications*, describes a practice that he calls *presencing*, the process of entering into a moment of stillness and letting go of any predetermined thoughts or actions in order to connect with what is present.[24] I have used the verb "seeing" to describe this practice, but "presencing" seems more descriptive. A teacher who is consciously practicing presencing lets go of agendas in order to be open and present to a child or class of children, pays close attention to what wants to happen, then trusts that intuition or presentiment and supports it with action. At such moments, we — the child and I or the children and I — decide together what to do next. Had I been fully practicing presencing when I responded to Chris, the outcome could have been transformative for both of us.

In my role as education director, I had frequent contact with the day's miscreants. A tall, intense eighth-grade boy was sent to the office because he had used profanity on the play yard in front of many younger children. His face was flushed. He was breathing heavily and near tears. I knew him as an honest young man who was quick to flare and lose his temper, so I got him a drink of water, sat in silence with him while he cooled down, and then asked him what had happened. He had climbed the fence around the play yard to retrieve a ball, and in the process, one of his friends had said some things that really upset him. He admitted that he had lost his temper and shouted some bad words.

We sat quietly for a moment, and then I asked him if he was interested in foiling future plots to make him lose his temper. He was surprised by my question, having expected the usual lecture about swearing, and he began to give me his full attention. I asked him if he had friends who thought it was fun to get him in trouble and suggested he might call their game the next time it happened. We then collaborated on creating a string of terrible-sounding, meaningless oaths that he could shout the next time he was angry. We enjoyed making up the words, and he left the office to go back to class with a grin on his face. I didn't see him again for this issue for the rest of the year. I like to think that he didn't need to use those nonsense words. The solution came out of our interaction, our being present to one another. I was as surprised by it as he was.

My practice through the years was an intention to see, understand, and respond appropriately to each child. I knew when I was successful by the child's response. This practice required that I trust myself, which was not always an easy task. It is much easier to follow a predetermined protocol or set of rules. Each time I took this risk, however, I supported my growth as well as the growth of my students. I became better able to go beyond sympathy or antipathy towards particular students and make an inclusive commitment to all those in my charge. I had to work harder to see and make connections with some students than with others, but that extra effort often proved to be the most fruitful.

My understanding of what it means to trust children evolved through my years as a Waldorf teacher. Steiner advised teachers in the first Waldorf school that the essential key to learning was not the curriculum, the pedagogy, or even the artistic work but the relationship between students and teachers. He told his teachers their primary task was to support the natural forces for learning at work in each child and to protect them from anything that might hinder or damage their development. Success was to be measured not by grades but by the amount of life force and enthusiasm attained by the students. This vital life force would provide the strength and courage necessary for young people to act on their ideals and begin to shape the world around them.[25] This is more easily said than done. Many factors affect modern children's development, from birthing practices to toxic exposures to social stressors such as poverty and homelessness. Neurological conditions such as autism are on the rise and profoundly affect children's ability to form attached relationships. Teachers may not be able to remove all these impediments, but they can dedicate themselves to ensuring that their students are seen and understood and receive the help they need.

A beginning first-grade teacher asked me to sit in to observe a little girl. This sweet child was paying attention, very focused and wanting to succeed, but when it came time to make a drawing or write a letter or a word in her book, she would flounder. Her pages were filled with indecipherable markings, and she was obviously upset as she watched her classmates accomplish tasks that seemed impossible to her. I had recently read about the Anat Baniel Method, a gentle, movement-based neuro-programming process developed by Feldenkrais practitioner Anat Baniel over decades of work with special-needs children.[26] I knew that a parent in our school had recently completed a training that prepared her to work with young children using this method. I suggested that the child's mother make an appointment. The next week, the teacher reported to me that after two therapeutic sessions, the child had picked up her pencil and drawn her first picture. She was so happy that she kept repeating," I can do it now! I can do it!" Removing impediments is seldom so magical, but this experience points to the neuroplasticity and responsiveness of children's brains if we can identify why they are stuck and find a way to support their growth.

Carrying this level of responsibility meant that I was never bored. It was essential that I had multiple years rather than months to observe and respond to my students' needs. Presencing helped me stay aware in the present moment and sustained my efforts when I felt tired or discouraged. I didn't try to articulate it to myself more than that.

Hannah, who had journeyed with me my last eight years as a teacher, wrote in my yearbook on my last day of teaching the quote that I used at the start of this chapter: "My hero is someone who wakes up every morning and loves the world all over again." Something much deeper and larger than my ego felt confirmed by those words. Perhaps that something is what my *qigong* teacher calls *shin* or heart-mind. How sad that we don't have a word in English for this source of love that sustains and connects us and is necessary for all of us if we are to grow and thrive as full human beings.

SUPPORT STRONG ATTACHMENT RELATIONSHIPS BETWEEN TEACHERS AND STUDENTS

1. **Schedule teachers for multiple-year relationships with one group of students.** Public education is not currently structured to support strong relationships between teachers and students. Few teachers have the opportunity to teach the same children for multiple years. All the insight and connection that has been garnered during the school year is dropped in June as the child goes on to the next teacher. This can be traumatic for children as well. I remember one of my sons weeping bitterly over having to say good-bye to his beloved third-grade teacher. Three or four years with a class should be a standard. Six to eight years is ideal during the elementary years. Teachers can make the case for multiple years with their classes if they can collaborate with colleagues and present a workable plan. Even two years is better than one!

   Teachers in Waldorf schools often opt for teaching the lower grades (first to fourth) or specializing in the upper grades (fifth to eighth). While this choice may reflect the teacher's particular talents or proclivities, it misses an opportunity for the teacher to grow and develop with the children. When students, who followed like ducklings in the lower grades, appear at the grade six door in attire that blatantly challenges the school dress code, they watch to see what their teacher will do. Will the relationship hold through a time of change and challenge? Will the teacher be able to change and grow with the class?

2. **Make *presencing* a practice for the faculty.** When the faculty and administration practice *presencing* in their meetings with each other and with parents, the educational system becomes more dynamic and transformative, more capable of supporting children and their families.

3. **Screen candidates carefully for personal issues.** Many beginning teachers struggle with their own attachment issues. Children are skilled at finding and pushing these reactive buttons. Teachers must be able to acknowledge such difficulties and understand how they affect classroom management. Such challenges may be overcome If administration is supportive and teachers are committed to personal growth. Phillip Riley, education professor at Australia Catholic University in Melbourne, Australia, wrote *Attachment Theory and the Teacher-Student Relationship: A Practical Guide for Teachers, Teacher Educators and School Leaders.*[27] Copies are available through Amazon.com. The Neufeld Institute also offers a number of courses for educators.[28] If a teacher is unable to form a strong attachment relationship with students, even with administrative support, they are in the wrong profession and should be replaced.

4. **Ensure that school discipline policies and procedures support teachers in their commitment to form strong attachment relationships with their classes.** Schools generally offer a mix of curative practices, pharmaceutical prescriptions, and behavior modification techniques. Discipline policies that outline rules and consequences leave little consideration for the needs of individual children and cause children to comply for the wrong reasons, i.e., to get a reward or avoid a consequence. Attachment theory addresses many of the questions that live in the gap between our professed aims and our daily implementations. What to do with a child who is too upset to comply with classroom protocols? Putting them outside the classroom is not a good option because it threatens attachment and increases

anxiety in an already anxious child. Having a safe, non-punitive place to go is one possibility, but having a comforting place within the classroom is even better. Find out what is causing a child to be upset or to misbehave, even if lessons have to wait. When a teacher treats every child with respect and attention, the whole class learns that they are safe and loved and how to treat one another. Conversely, a teacher who shames, reacts out of anger, and is punitive or sarcastic to any child loses the respect and trust of the entire class.

5. **Collaborate (faculty, administration, and parents) to ensure discipline policies are in line with core values.** Student behavior guidelines were the result of such a collaboration and were posted for students, parents, and all members of our school community. The following statement was sent to all parents.

Expectations of Students

All children want to do well and hope to succeed in school. If they are firmly attached to their teachers and are supported by their families, they will do their best to please us and to follow our guidelines for behavior in class and on the school grounds.

Student Behavior Guidelines

Each classroom is posted with the following guidelines:

Be respectful: Students will learn to speak and act respectfully to their teachers and each other. We will also respect our work by doing our best and taking care of our books and our classroom tools. We will respect our classrooms by keeping them tidy and clean and our grounds by keeping them free from litter. We will take pride in our school and do what we can to make it a beautiful and peaceful place. The adults will model this process in the school as they talk with each other and with the children. Expectations are different for first graders than for sixth graders, but the message is the same. We will strive to treat each other fairly and with respect even when we disagree or are angry.

Be responsible: Students will do their best to be at school on time and to be prompt for their classes. They will complete their assignments and turn them in on time. They will finish their classwork in the time allotted for it. When they make mistakes or forget to comply with the guidelines, students will take responsibility for their actions and make amends. They will come to school appropriately dressed and ready for the activities of the day and weather.

Be kind: Students will learn to care for each other. Through buddy classes and through sharing at assemblies, in classrooms and on the playground, children will learn to help each other and to cooperate.

These guidelines represent an ideal and an intention. We understand that children who feel accepted, seen, and valued are most able to comply. When children are disruptive, disrespectful, or upset, we see such behavior as communication and strive to understand what is behind it. Is the child overtired or hungry? Is the child worried? Is the family under unusual stress due to illness, economic challenges, divorce, or all of the above? Has the child experienced significant trauma? Is there a sensory or perceptual imbalance that is impeding learning? Is the child being picked on by other children? Are our adult learning expectations inappropriate or poorly presented? These are only a few of the questions that we might ask. Finding the answers to such questions is far more effective than punishment in changing children's behavior. Teachers will help children find appropriate ways to make amends if they have been unkind, damaged school property, or disrupted learning for themselves or other students.

Children who continue to act out aggressively or disrupt classes will be worked with individually to help them be more successful socially and academically. There are occasions when we recommend that a child should leave the classroom to work one on one with a learning specialist. An extremely upset child may need to go home for the day to rest and then return. This should not be viewed as a punishment.

Occasionally, older students may commit serious breaches of the guidelines by acting or speaking violently or by bringing illegal objects or substances onto campus. In such cases, the student may be suspended. The administration, teacher, and parents will meet with the student to ensure that such behavior will not be repeated, and that the student is getting the help needed to be able to comply.

Our school is part of a culture that has traditionally meted out harsh punishments for student misbehavior in the belief that such consequences will frighten students into compliance. This approach has failed. Failure or expulsion from school puts children on a fateful path, often to incarceration. Our school is committed to seeing the value and worth of every child. It is this commitment, not standardized testing, that ensures that "no child is left behind."

6. **Reinforce school policies through ongoing parent education.** Parents feel supported and are more open to learning new parenting skills when teachers consistently model supportive ways of responding to student needs. After several years of working with attachment-based learning principles, I observed more cohesion in the faculty, more support from the parents, and far fewer crises with the children.

For parents: Embrace the challenge and growth involved in the essential relationships you have with your child(ren) and support the natural activities described in each chapter of this book. Investigate the Neufeld Institute and attachment parenting. *Hold On to Your Kids* by Gordon Neufeld and Gabor Maté is a great support for parents in this challenging time. *Your Child's Growing Mind* by Jane Healy helps to scale expectations to children's developmental needs. Independence is achieved by children who have been deeply respected and securely held through childhood and adolescence.

. . . . .

In summary, children learn from teachers they trust, from adults who make them feel safe, do not trap them in labels, and orient them positively to the world. When parents, teachers, and administrators form a supportive circle around children, learning happens for everyone. This circle of relationships is the crucible in which the arts, stories, games, studies, and rhythms of the day, week, and year nurture the growth of each child while giving birth to a dynamic community of learners.

Chapter Three

Build Community

The healthy social life is found when, in the mirror of each human soul, the whole community finds its reflection, and when, in the community, there lives the strength and virtue of each one.

—Rudolf Steiner

This verse, spoken at the beginning of faculty meetings in Waldorf schools, describes a dynamic essential to healthy social life, a balance that must be continually in motion between our responsibilities to each other and our individual aspirations. Communities are a natural extension of primary attachment relationships. The simplest definition I have found for community is "a group of people who care about each other." Community is our primary resource for collaboration, sharing, emotional support, and safety.

An increasing number of us are no longer born into such communities, but our need for this kind of attachment is innate and urgent. Modern libertarians seem to forget that strong communities are important for survival and ignore the irony implicit in a "cult of the individual." On the other side, communities that do not allow for difference or deviance from a set of qualities or beliefs are repressive and offer security at the cost of personal freedom. Watching the political sideshows of recent election campaigns, I am struck by how much confusion and division there is in our society on this issue. Yet, I do not recall a single serious discussion of this topic in all of my years in school.

I sent a Facebook shout-out to some of my former students, soliciting their thoughts and memories about our class community. I received a response from Joey in Berlin, where he had moved after graduating from college. Two of his former classmates, Hannah and Max, had recently traveled from Tel Aviv and London, respectively, and spent the New Year's holiday with him. Joey wrote:

> *Speaking from the present, and especially since distance is currently so salient, this has been largely a time of reflecting and self-collecting. In addition to the aspects of myself that still resonate with the influence of my former classmates, it has been powerful to experience the pieces of me that they have been holding onto. I particularly noticed this when spending time with Hannah and Max. They remember me in a way that is hard for me to grasp by myself through time and that is also somehow different from what my nuclear family can relate to me, perhaps in that there is less familial bias.*

Joey speaks of being surprised by the pieces of himself that Hannah and Max reflect back to him. Their memories enhance and extend his own, allowing him to see himself through their eyes. Seeing and being seen are formative forces essential to growth and the unfolding of capacities. Mirroring by a trusted adult is amplified exponentially as children begin to form a community in which the strength and virtue of each child are mirrored and celebrated by the group.

I believe that it was my intention — to strive to see each child as clearly as possible and to reflect that seeing not only to the child but to the whole group of children — that sparked a healthy community to develop over the years in our classroom. It was also the perception — *This teacher sees and appreciates my child* — that formed a supportive community of parents around the children. That we had eight years to build this trust was significant. How sad and short-sighted that school programs take for granted that teachers should be grade-level-curriculum specialists instead of specialists in understanding the particular children in their care. It takes time to gain the trust and respect of children and develop insight into what they need. It was a tremendous gift to travel with a group of children through all the changes of childhood into adolescence, knowing them and their families better and more deeply at each stage.

There were many developmental challenges through the years. Cliques formed and dissolved, conflicts emerged and were mediated, habits and patterns of social interaction surfaced and then were transformed. Community in our class was dynamic, never a given. It grew and evolved with the children while they were with me and has continued for many of them through their teenage years into adulthood. We built community by sharing stories, experiences, and adventures and by developing an appreciation for each other's abilities. Lily expresses this sensibility when she writes about the importance of the arts to her education:

> *I remember being so overjoyed when I saw a friend who struggled in certain academic classes excel so completely in creating the most oval and perfectly sanded wooden egg during woodworking. Or seeing others who often couldn't sit still for more than a minute, get so deeply focused on the beeswax bear they were forming. There were others still whose writing or math skills were unbeatable, yet when it came to knitting socks, they became very frustrated. For some, their paintings and poems were as beautiful as their essays, and yet, even for them, being in these different weaving, pottery, and sewing classes instilled compassion for others who were having a hard time, patience for the process of learning a new skill, focus, determination. It also offered the space for some people to step back and allow others to shine, giving people confidence in their own abilities.*

Our community was the sheath in which capacities for empathy and a sense of shared responsibility could grow. Some children carried this impulse more strongly than others, but everyone operated within its protection. It gave us identity as a group so that the children could say "we" and speak for each other as well as themselves. This group autonomy grew with the children and had a life of its own, welcoming and shaping new class members to its ethic.

Several moments rise in my memory. The class traveled to a neighboring school in fifth grade to participate in the Medieval Games: jousting, tug of war, racing, and archery. The next day, the girls were grumbling during lunch about the way that the girls from another school had treated them and each other. When I asked what was different, Hannah responded, "We're Mrs. Cummings's girls; we would never treat each other that *way!*"

A dispute broke out during a game of kickball. Sixth grade is a time for wide emotional swings, and our games were often a stage for these dramas. Joey became very upset with the group and left the game, going to the other side of the field in tears. Everything stopped, and Ami looked at me and said, "It's okay, Mrs. Cummings. I'll take care of him. I understand how he feels." We returned to the classroom, and Ami sat in the grass with her arm around Joey. They spoke well into the next class period, and by the time they came back, they were both smiling. Nothing more needed to be said.

You have already met Jasper in fourth-grade painting class. He was still somewhat socially isolated as we started the middle school years and would often walk around the periphery of our playground during breaks. This pattern continued until Nate began to seek him out, saying, "Hey, Jasper, come play four square with me," pulling him into the game and encouraging him. Other children picked up the cue and began to do the same. Soon, they were all involving Jasper in their activities, calling him out, choosing him first. It was wonderful to see the change in him, the joy and pleasure in his eyes, the transformation in his carriage and gait. He was still his quirky, unique self but was now embedded safely in a circle of friends. This is what community can offer. Everyone benefits when there is a healthy social life that celebrates the strength and virtue of each member.

Everyone has also experienced the absence of healthy community. Other dynamics often rule in classrooms. Children who are not firmly led by the adults in their lives or who have been mistreated or abused often try to take charge by bullying or excluding their peers and creating fear and trauma for others.

A girl entered my class when I was in seventh grade. Malnourished and pale, she wore hand-me-down clothes and shoes and was very shy, speaking seldom. Her name was Florabelle, and some children cruelly christened her Fleabag. I was not part of the group that taunted her, but we all excluded her, fearing that if we didn't, we would become outcasts, too. My family moved at the end of the eighth grade, and I learned the following year that Florabelle had committed suicide. I remember the shock and the guilt I felt with the consciousness that there might have been a different outcome if I had mustered the courage to stand up for her. I told my students this cautionary tale, urging them not to make my mistake. Building a healthy social life in a school can be a matter of life and death. Children who are excluded are at high risk. Children who are allowed to exclude or torment others poison the social sphere and stunt their own potential, developing sociopathology instead of compassion in their adult lives.

Developing a healthy social life in the classroom should be a priority, given its educational significance. This means taking advantage of opportunities that the children present, even if it means disrupting lesson plans. I remember one class in particular when the students came in after recess and had a hard time settling down. When it was clear that most of them were not listening to me, I stopped and said, "What's going on? Did something happen at recess that we should talk about?" I don't remember the specifics of the situation, but I remember the energy and relief with which the students told me their various stories about what had happened. We spent a productive hour resolving the situation together, a far more potent lesson than the one I had prepared.

At the beginning of our seventh-grade year, a social crisis emerged. Two girls, Genny and Linnea, who had been close friends for years, had a falling out triggered primarily by different rates of sexual maturation. They were both strong personalities, and soon, the class was unhappily divided into two groups — those who supported Genny and those who supported Linnea. Beginning in first grade, our class had collaborated on rules that outlined how we were to treat each other. These rules were no longer adequate. After several failed attempts to help the girls resolve their differences, I took a less direct approach. I excused Genny and Linnea from classwork and asked them if they would work together to write new protocols for class behavior that would be more appropriate for seventh and eighth graders. They agreed and were absent from class for most of the day. When they returned, the class unanimously accepted the new rules they presented. The crisis was over. The girls followed the protocol they had written, and their differences were no longer an issue for the group.

Children who have experienced the support and encouragement of a loving community carry that understanding with them as they go out into the larger world. They find new circles and reach out to others even as they maintain old friendships and associations. I am struck as I follow my former students on Facebook by how interconnected many of them are, how they support each other in their various explorations. Social media is an amazing tool for maintaining contact, particularly if it is based on real knowledge and understanding of the other. I can see the outlines of a new community that is no longer based on proximity but on shared purpose and vision, a community that spans the world.

Again, from Joey:

One of my most rewarding recent experiences with community came from my semester at the Moscow Art Theater. The ensemble was one of the primary structural and pedagogical foci of the program. Working in a group every day to develop projects and formulate new work involved an intense and raw interaction of egos, largely, I believe, because we were engaging in creative and artistic — and therefore inherently and wholly subjective — work and practice. It was hard, and tense, and frustrating, and arduous. By the end, however, the trust and intimacy we had developed, together with the efforts we had put toward functioning well as a group, led us to an incredibly free and trusting level of communication... Herein lies part of the great value of communities like the Waldorf class you guided and my program in Moscow: by feeling known and supported, I feel much more free to take risks, trusting that my actions will be understood and judged according to who I am. If I then fail, it is simply the outcome of a risk Joey took within the context of all my successes and failures, as opposed to a failure in the void with my name stamped on it.

My eight-year journey with this group of children was both healing and empowering. I had experienced tastes of community potential in my work in theater and with students over the years, but I did not fully understand the dynamics of building such a community. To do so, I had to accept that I was not the only one who was offering a mirror. The children were my mirror. The more I trusted that reflection, the more easily we charted our way together. As Joey expressed so clearly, we are able to take creative risks and be resilient when our efforts fail if we feel securely held and seen rather than judged.

Parents formed a second ring of community around this class of children. I knew how important it was for parents to be informed and involved. We had a class meeting or workshop once a month, and I wrote Sunday-night letters describing key events or discoveries of the past week and alerting the parents about what was to come. In turn, they helped in the classroom, drove on field trips, spent weeks in the wilds camping with us, and were involved in our numerous endeavors — class plays, festivals, athletic contests, and performances.

Do you sense the backstory in this short summary? It was a continuous education for all of us. My greatest challenge was learning to listen openly to concerns — to just listen and focus on making sure that I fully understood what parents were saying instead of reacting or trying to correct misperceptions. I realized in the process that the parents needed to feel seen and heard as much as their children. The parents, in turn, had to learn to be forthright (no parking lot conspiracies!) and to respect boundaries. At times, emails went furiously back and forth, but on the whole, these caring adults made a strong circle of love and support around the whole class.

We built community from first grade onward by making agreements and keeping them. We made agreements about media exposure, birthday parties, and sleepovers. We stayed with these issues until we had a strong consensus about our community rules and guidelines that allowed parents to trust each other even when they didn't agree. I also created opportunities for them to know each other at a deeper level. I introduced them to the vagaries of the nine-year change and adolescence by having them each recall and share something that they remembered feeling or thinking at that age.[29] When they finished sharing, there was a sense of relief and discovery: *Oh, that's what is going on!* A shared commitment to the process and the trust that we could work out our differences without threatening relationship grew over time. When it truly "takes a village," the learning is deep and wide for everyone involved.

Consistent and thoughtful communication is the key to forming a community of parents around a class. In addition to weekly newsletters, I wrote a summary of what had been accomplished during the year and a description of each child's progress instead of giving grades. Formative assessment, an ongoing picture of each child that includes their strengths and challenges, is worth the extra time and effort. The assessment helped me review the year and chart the progress of each student on multiple fronts. I was also able to build trust with parents by allowing them to question and discuss my observations. This was the only form of assessment that I used until sixth grade, when I began to grade quizzes and tests to help the children make a transition to grading in high school. I do not think that grading, in general, enhances learning. Teacher feedback and comments are far more effective and meaningful to students and parents. Here is an example:

> Dear Michael and Shelley,
>
> Our little sprout has been growing and learning and turning into a beautiful flower! How lovely that Annamalka feels this about herself. Gratitude is a high moral quality which she carries quite naturally in her being. Being a recipient of Annamalka's gratitude feels like a blessing.
>
> Third grade has been a year of steady progress and growth for your child. At the end of the year, she is truly blooming in many areas at once, social as well as academic.
>
> Annamalka reads well above her grade level with good vocabulary and comprehension. She has a delightful sense of humor and relishes nuances and subtle meanings. She tends to hold her book very close to her face, however, and I would recommend that she have her vision checked by a developmental ophthalmologist. (There are several in our area). She may need to work with eye exercises to strengthen her eyes to work together. She still confuses some letters as well, saying p for b. Some of the challenges that made early academic learning difficult for her are still faintly present and frustrate her. She is strongly motivated to excel and wants to do her work perfectly. Why can't she just naturally spell all the words right?!
>
> Annamalka likes to write stories and descriptions. She is very imaginative and sometimes brings an unusual depth of insight or understanding to her expression. Left to her own devices, she does not punctuate but goes on in a stream of consciousness very much like

her breathless, excited speech. We have been working to slow her down and to bring more form so that others will be able to understand what she is saying.

I was so pleased with Annamalka's performance in the play. This year, she did very well with her part and seemed to enjoy being the "only" sister in a stable of brothers. The clarity and passion which she is bringing now to her birthday verse in the morning tells me that Annamalka has arrived 100% and is standing on the earth with confidence and enthusiasm.

Annamalka has also made strong progress in arithmetic. She initially had difficulty learning her math facts but has become very motivated to do so. She is in process with both her addition and multiplication facts and would profit by working on these this summer. One way to practice is with mental math, starting with simple number combinations and making them gradually more challenging. (3x4+4÷2=?). She also knows which tables she needs to work on. Her understanding of the four processes—addition, subtraction, multiplication, and division—is still in process, and she is held back by being unsure of her tables. She could use practice with multiplication and division particularly. Playing games, like cards, that involve manipulating numbers might also be fun for her.

Drawing is often a time of much hilarity. Annamalka is brave in what she attempts and is often amused by the result. She enjoys making pictures and painting, particularly when I allow the children to make their own interpretations. She loved the hands-on projects of third grade, particularly the cooking block. She often helped me on Friday to make challah and was very responsible about timing the baking and organizing every detail. I enjoyed watching her on the farm trip: her pleasure in the surroundings, the animals and the plants, and her resilience in spite of the heat and the hard work. She has basically seemed to be a very happy and vibrant child this spring.

Socially, Annamalka has found a soul mate in Gwen. Although this relationship was fairly exclusive for much of the year, it is now softening and opening up as Gwen makes other contacts in the class. That Annamalka is allowing this without obvious distress is a sign of her new maturity. Instead of retreating into the safe imaginary worlds of mouse houses and Planet BX, Annamalka now spends many recesses playing kickball with the most active core of the class. She plays hard, runs fast, and is surprisingly athletic. She is much more engaged socially with all of the girls and many of the boys.

Getting Annamalka to chat less has been a challenge, particularly because Annamalka also talks to herself. She talks herself through activities as a strategy that supports her through little challenges. Alone, this is no problem. But in a large class, it can become annoying to the children around her, who are also trying to focus. She has been trying to do better, and her infractions at this point are seldom deliberate or stubborn. The testing of teachers that we talked about earlier in the year has dwindled. It's clear that Annamalka wants to behave and perform as well as she can—and she is!

I just enjoy being around this funny, sensitive, intuitive girl. She has made a very comfortable nest for herself in my heart. What a joy to be able to share her this way with you. Thanks for your steady support and appreciation. And thank you, Shelley, for the magnificent performance in the kitchen on the farm trip.

Field trips, particularly ones that last for multiple days, can make or break class community. I put a lot of effort and planning into each trip so that the parents and the children could relax and no time would be wasted. One such adventure was particularly magical.

The fourth graders were camped in the reconstructed gold rush town of North Bloomfield at Malakoff Diggings State Park in the foothills of the Sierras. The children were dressed in appropriate costumes, and several parents and volunteers had spent the day leading them through craft activities: candle making, blacksmithing, woodworking, cooking, and tin smithing, during which they designed, punched, and assembled lanterns for their candles.

The following description is from a letter I wrote to the parents who were unable to come with us:

> Imagine a great iron kettle filled with melted wax and the children going in a slow circle around an adjacent tree, dipping their wicks again and again until the candles began to take form. Focus, concentration, and industry were amazing.
>
> They were all finished by 5:30 pm, just in time for delicious stew complete with dumplings and apple crisp. After dinner, we were regaled by old Alkali—a miner who lived to tell us his tale. He is one of the best storyteller-musicians I have ever experienced. As the sun began to set, we went down a little path through thickets into an even more beautiful and pristine meadow and danced the Virginia Reel to Alkali's fiddle and Leslie's calling. Coming back along this path with their lanterns alight, a number of children began spontaneously to sing, "Softly, softly through the night," their kindergarten Advent song. As they sang, they moved out into a big spiral, which closed in and then opened out again. (Their movement teacher, Barbara Newman, would have been so pleased!)

They ended in a big, perfect circle where they shared the thoughts and ideas that inspired their lantern designs. During the sharing, I felt the fullness of each child—relaxed, happy, and fully present to one another and to us. One of the parents whispered, "It doesn't get any better than this!" My feelings exactly.

Many of my students spent ten years together at the Marin Waldorf School. By the end of eighth grade, they were ready to explore new horizons, and I felt confident that they were well prepared. Our emotions were high. We spent a week hiking and snorkeling on Catalina Island, ending with a challenging ropes course in Santa Barbara. Genny told the graduation audience about her experience on the last day of this trip.

On our last day, our group formed a circle. The activity required each person in the class to stand in the center of the circle one at a time as their fellow classmates showered them with love by describing, in turn, the qualities we loved best about each other. For instance, Annamalka told Lily Rubin that she is a smiler. Ms. Cummings told James he is wise. I told Jack he is kind. Linnea told Michael Gilbertson he is hilarious. Kaleb told Mr. Ganz that he is the best dad ever. (I just sobbed over that one.) I realized that with each comment, more and more tears were flowing from my eyes.

I realized how much I was going to miss my class, my family, and with each tear, my resistance to entering the circle only mounted. To be seen in the full throes of emotion, believe it or not, that's what's hard for me, for I do care so deeply, and sometimes the vulnerability is just too much. The first person to address me was our trip coordinator, Jeff. He told me that I make a very good first impression. I realized gratefully that, yes, this is one thing my Waldorf education has taught me—to relate well to people. Max told me that I am everyone's best friend. Meleah told me I am funny. In that circle, I realized I was able to let all my insecurities show and still know that I was loved and held. In that circle, I didn't have to be big, or funny, or wild to receive all that I did. Even in my most bare state—tears—I was accepted by the people who knew and loved me just for who I am. That circle was my graduation—not just a graduation into high school but a graduation into life. With this class, I could have eyes as red as cherries from crying and a handful of tissues, and they will still see me as their Genny. I think that all of us, in a profound way, have realized what I am speaking about today. This is what I will carry with me into high school and into my future, wherever that will be.

STEPS TO BUILDING STRONG CLASS
AND SCHOOL COMMUNITIES

1. **Schedule elementary-age children to be with the same group and teacher over a number of years.** If teachers change, keep the group of children together. This is their community, and it is precious and important for their learning. In large high schools, community can be built in special programs within the larger school. Students can be grouped in cohorts that move through some classes together and meet to share experiences, discuss problems, etc. These cohorts can be interest based, offering specialized classes in science, the arts, etc. The primary goal is to ensure that students don't drop through the cracks or become marginalized or isolated in a large student body. This approach also supports innovation beyond traditional subject-based curriculum. A school within a school, for example, might emphasize project-based learning or the performing arts.[30]

2. **Involve students in decision and rulemaking up and down the grades.** Students must be allowed to make mistakes and learn from the process. Regular class meetings, led initially by the teacher and progressively by students, develop the social skills necessary for a democratic society. Students learn to listen to one another, to collaborate, to disagree respectfully, to come to a consensus, and to uphold the decisions they make. This activity not only builds community in the classroom but also teaches students how to be effective citizens.

3. **Implement programs that teach social skills and awareness.** I recently discovered the Inquiry Institute, established by Marilee Adams, a former teacher. She developed a program that teaches students to identify whether they are using "judger mind" or "learner mind." This program teaches explicitly and effectively what I tried to teach implicitly and is an excellent support for personal and social growth.[31]

4. **Hold regular parent meetings and keep parents informed to build a strong parent circle around a class or program.** At best, these meetings should manifest adult versions of the same social principles that the children are learning, modeling mutual respect, collaboration, and respect for group decisions. Remember that parents, like children, love good stories and playful, creative activities. The time it takes to write a weekly newsletter and plan parent meetings and workshops is time well spent.

5. **Involve parents in activities and field trips and invite them to help with planning and decision making.** Parents can also assist in teaching classes in their areas of expertise or talent. Collaboration builds strong community. Parent support is essential for successful field trips and nature excursions. So much more becomes possible when the load is shared.

6. **Promote a healthy social life through faculty meetings that build mutual respect and consensual support for decisions and protocols.** Children model trusted adults. If the adults trust

and work well together, the children will, too. This should be a priority for all teachers and educators — to model a healthy social life in which the whole faculty can find its reflection in each teacher and each teacher feels supported and encouraged by the community. This is always a work in progress, but it is wonderful practice for living in a real democracy.

For Parents: Parents are essential members of each class and school community. Share your expertise, organizational skills, and creativity. Building a strong circle of parents around a class of children supports their sense of safety and engagement and creates a continuum between home and school. Parents also provide support for each other's families through challenging times. Plan ahead so that you can participate, if possible, in trips and excursions. It does take a village!

· · · · ·

A healthy social life cannot form in a competitive atmosphere that divides members into winners and losers. I hold our educational system partially accountable for the polarization and discord that is currently paralyzing our government and dispiriting our citizenry. Students are taught to compete for grades, for acceptance into college, for jobs. Too few are rewarded, too many carry heavy burdens of debt, and tragically, too many are labeled as failures.

I believe that the current explosion of violent acts, both self- and other-inflicted, would most effectively be addressed by an educational system dedicated to developing the worth of each child.

The best way I know to accomplish this feat is to build strong, healthy communities around and within each class. For example, clear communication between parents and teachers in the primary grades is essential to ensure that everyone understands and supports a developmental, stress-free approach to teaching reading. I remember hearing about a grandmother who expressed concern at Christmas that her first-grade granddaughter was not reading yet. Grandma informed her that her cousin, also in first grade, could read her favorite books and asked if that upset her. The girl, who was in a Waldorf school, told her grandmother that she wasn't worried. "She may be able to read, Grandma, but she doesn't even know what the letters mean."

Chapter Four

How Children Become Fluent Readers

We dance with light feet and enjoy our selfs and imagine we are flying. Then we go to bed and dream of our dancing. We are awakened by the morning him self and he takes us to his castle. Inside we go to the courtyard. There we see a beautiful malorn tree in bloom. Faintly it shines as if it was the sun shapd as a tree. The end.

—James, age eight

A copy of this writing by second-grader James hangs on the wall above my desk. He gave it to me as a "get well" gift when illness kept me home for a few days. Each time I read it, I am delighted. This ability to share our experiences, dreams, and thoughts with one another through language is at the core of our humanity. Nurturing such capacities was one of my primary responsibilities as a teacher.

James's story also provided valuable information about James. The images that he vividly described were stimulated by J.R. Tolkien's *The Hobbit,* a story that his parents were reading to him. Inspired by Tolkien, James was not only writing his own story, but he was also mastering figurative language—the effective use of personification and simile—many grades ahead of schedule. I did not have to give shy James a test to know that he was becoming a fluent reader and writer.

I am focusing on how and when to teach reading in this chapter because learning to read is the gateway for all subsequent academic instruction. The degree of ease and pleasure of accomplishment that children experience in the process of learning to read determines how they feel about themselves as students and how they feel about school. Emotional and neurological patterns, once established, are not easy to reverse or to heal. I received students in my classes who were emotionally and intellectually damaged by the stress of early school experiences. I encountered high school students, in Waldorf as well as public high schools, who did not receive the special help they needed as young children to become fluent readers. Being able to read may not be a prerequisite for being an intelligent, wise, and gifted human being, but it is a crucial skill for full participation in our society.

Young children are word sponges, full of curiosity and pride as they gain understanding of the world around them by expanding their vocabularies. This daily accomplishment is not a rote learning process. They learn by listening. They learn by imitating. The richer and more omnipresent language is in their surroundings, and the more stories they hear, the stronger their language skills, imaginations, and memories become. Children's natural capacities for language acquisition are remarkable. They master complex syntax and the basic grammatical constructions of English long before they go to school. They learn subject-verb agreement, verb tenses, and proper use of adjectives and adverbs by kindergarten. First and second graders can remember the lines of a play or a poem "by heart" after hearing them only a few times — faster than older children and much faster than adults.

This ability to learn languages is our legacy as human beings. For most of history, humans have participated in oral cultures that pass down knowledge through stories and teachings. These stories are the repositories of wisdom and information needed for survival, memorized and then passed on through countless generations. In the process, humans developed powerful inherent mind tools for organizing and retaining information. These innate abilities activate as children learn to communicate and strive to understand the world around them. The determination and patience of young learners can be confirmed by every parent and grandparent who has observed their progress with amazement and pride. A salient question might be to ask what stops them from learning when they get to school, given the urgency of this natural drive. How is it that many students, who have spent approximately thirteen thousand hours in school over a twelve-year period, graduate with weak basic skills, unable to read critically or write with clarity?

An article by Colin Wells, "From Memory to Innovation: The Vowel Revolution in the Making of the Modern Mind," offers an important clue.[32] Literate culture was born in Ancient Greece with the creation of the first modern alphabet, complete with vowels and consonants. Prior to the Greek alphabet, reading and writing belonged to small, elite groups of scribes. Cognitive disciplines like philosophy, history, and science grew as individual readers were able, for the first time, to study, critique, and improve on the thoughts of others. This profound shift sparks the beginning of Western civilization. It still resonates around the world as developed literate societies interact with traditional oral cultures. Every child who starts school stands at the threshold of this challenge.

Teachers understand that most children need significant support to make this leap from their natural, intuitive ways of learning oral language to achieving literacy and the abstraction required for critical thinking. We are not born ready to read. Children must learn how to decode shapes into sounds and words, remember those words correctly in written as well as spoken form, and then understand their meaning. This challenging task requires integrated feedback from both hemispheres of the brain.

Recent brain research verifies what teachers and parents know from experience—that children's brains mature at different rates and that timing is critical to successful learning. Most children who are pushed to read before the age of seven rely primarily on right-hemisphere brain processes that mature first. Their primary tactic will be to memorize sight words, a tiring task that can interfere with comprehension of meaning. If children see only words on a page and those words do not stimulate inner pictures, they will not grasp the meaning or be able to remember what they have read. The frustrated child does not understand why they are failing if they can successfully identify words.

Formal reading instruction should start when the child's left hemisphere is more developed and the two hemispheres are able to communicate smoothly with each other. Then children are better prepared to sound out unfamiliar words phonetically as well as remember some of them visually, a much less arduous process. At a magical point, their intuitive language skills also activate, and they begin to read text with the ease and understanding they bring to oral language.

Children have different timetables for reading readiness. A small number of children start to read on their own before school. Most girls are ready to begin reading between the ages of six and eight. Boys generally mature a year later, between the ages of seven and nine. The age at which a child becomes a reader does not affect later fluency or academic performance except for the children who are pushed to read before they are neurologically ready.[33]

Research shows that brain maturation is supported and enhanced by physical movement and play.[34] Historically, kindergartens have provided a year of play and socialization that prepared young children for later academic tasks. Current testing programs pressure schools to push reading, math, and academic worksheets into kindergartens, arguing that this will help students meet later grade-level expectations. Schools that implement such a policy ignore brain science and practical wisdom. They force young children to forgo the creative play and physical activity that is their primary developmental need in order to do extra work on activities that they are not developmentally ready to perform. What does that level of stress do to their neurological, physical, and emotional development? Dr. Jane Healy, whose book *Your Child's Growing Mind* was my essential guide as I switched from leading high school seminars to teaching young children, is very clear on the subject:

Studies show that four-, five-, and six-year-olds in heavily "academic" classes tend to become less creative and more anxious — without gaining significant advantage over their peers. Youngsters in well-structured "play-oriented" schools develop more positive attitudes toward learning along with better ultimate skill development.... Give your child the gift of patience for the broad-based mental experiences that will underlie joyous learning throughout life. Teaching specific academic skills before the levels of sensory reception and association are in place is like trying to build a large penthouse on an apartment building before the intermediate floors are completed. It may look good for a while, but eventually you're in for a collapse. Childhood is a process, not a product, and so is learning.[35]

The collapse that Dr. Healy warns us to expect can have lifelong repercussions. Children who are confronted with tasks they are not ready to accomplish lose confidence in their abilities. They want desperately to please their teachers and parents and are emotionally devastated when they fail. They begin to believe that they are stupid. Such students may go into flight-or-fight mode when asked a question or given a test. They may shut down emotionally and intellectually to protect themselves. Such emotional states block their normal development and confirm children's fears as they fall further behind their classmates. No child should have to experience this scenario.

Waldorf schools address this issue by protecting play-based kindergartens and recommending that children start first grade at age seven. First graders practice daily physical activities that strengthen and stimulate neurological readiness for reading and writing. These physical exercises engage opposite arms and legs and involve crawling and jumping or throwing and passing balls. Fine muscle activities that use both hands, such as knitting and playing the flute, further support the integration of the right and left hemispheres of the brain. Children whose hemispheres are integrating can reach across their midlines to pick up objects. They can write sentences from left to right without struggling. Their eyes can move smoothly across the page without jumping at the midpoint.

By the end of the year, my twenty-seven first graders were accomplished knitters and flute players whose brains were primed to start reading text. They were familiar with the sounds of the alphabet and could write simple words and sentences. Some children, mostly girls, had begun to read on their own. We began to read together in second grade, and by the end of the academic year, most children were reading fluently. If reading had been introduced in kindergarten, many of these children would have struggled and experienced fear of failure instead of the joy of accomplishment. The stress of that process might have closed the door to reading for pleasure, thus stunting the development of imagination and memory. Our first-grade year was filled with stories, artistic activities, outings, and creative play. I don't believe that my early readers were in any way "held back." Each day felt full of discovery.

Children enjoy and are primed to listen to stories. I told my students daily stories that they would retell verbally and illustrate the following day. This activity strengthens imagination and memory as well as building vocabulary. I introduced the alphabet, and we printed the letters and practiced the sounds each letter makes. They enjoyed copying the letters and writing simple words that they could illustrate. They also enjoyed dictating what they wanted me to write and then trying to read it back to themselves. Dictating and then copying their own stories was an engaging and empowering process for some children that led effortlessly to reading.

Ami had written such a story for her first-grade class. This was not an assignment. She asked about spelling many of the words, and I wrote them on the board for her. When she finished the story, I suggested that she share it with her classmates. She stood up and, her eyes dancing, began to read out loud what she had written. Midway, she stopped, her mouth opened wide, and she exclaimed, "I'm reading! I can read!" And everyone clapped. This shining moment of discovery could not have been engineered. Ami inspired other children to write stories, and soon, a number of children were helping each other spell words and reading their stories to one another.

Ami's felicitous discovery and its encouraging challenge to her classmates demonstrate how writing can be a natural bridge to reading. I recounted a similar event in my weekly parent letter toward the end of first grade.

> We had been working with a poem we had memorized, copying a few lines a day in our lesson books. When we finished, I told the children they could make up sentences using the words that they recognized. Intense activity and hilarity ensued. Then hands waved in the air. Could they read their sentences aloud to everyone? I agreed, and one at a time, they stood and read their sentences to the class.
>
> When they were finished, I asked them if they realized what they had just done. A moment of silence. Then a voice: "WE WERE READING!" I love this way of teaching. Some of the children are, in fact, reading, and others are beginning to sound words out with interest. There is no pressure, I hope, to do so in class or at home. Some children are simply not ready, and pushing them could cause future difficulty and present frustration.
>
> I hope that we can have a discussion around this issue at our next parent meeting. Meanwhile, all the children are becoming more adept with oral language and better able to discriminate sounds.

A teacher's primary task is to support and inspire children where they are developmentally. Kindergarten and first-grade children love fairy tales; they live into them, imagining them intensely and acting them out through their play. But after age seven, fairy tales begin to lose their luster. The children then begin to be more engaged by stories about young people who are faced with and overcome challenges. Developmental growth continues with a similar pattern as students move up the grades.

If you ask third-grade children about a story they have read, they will tell you the story, sometimes with amazingly accurate detail. They cannot tell you what the theme of the story is or analyze its characters. The independent capacity to think abstractly about what a story means or whether or not it was well written does not begin to blossom for most children until early adolescence. Pushing such analysis into the lower grades as the Common Core test does is an inappropriate exercise that hinders development by increasing anxiety and stress.

Junior high students can learn to write informational, five-paragraph essays that recount what they have read or researched, but most students are not able to write inductive essays that develop and support a point of view until they are sophomores or juniors. Again, asking them to do so prematurely impedes their intellectual progress in the long run.

Waldorf's model for structuring education to support the developmental needs and abilities of young children is not only confirmed by recent brain research but is successful even as measured by standardized tests. In 2017, Stanford University completed a thorough, multiple-year evaluation of Alice Birney, a K–8 Waldorf public charter school in Sacramento, California.

> *Quantitative analysis of student record data as well as qualitative analysis of interviews with Birney graduates reveals that Birney successfully supports students' development. Birney produces greater gains for its low-income and African American and Latino students than for its school population as a whole. Birney students demonstrate low transiency and suspension rates, positive student-achievement outcomes, and graduate from high school at high rates... Interviews with graduates reveal that their K–8 experiences support their continued growth and learning orientation through*

high school and college. In particular, graduates report they approached their continued education with the assumption that their voices were worth hearing and sharing, be it with peers or their classroom teachers, even if they were taking a minority or unorthodox position. Driven to pursue personally relevant educational interests, for the purpose of self-improvement and curiosity, they did not fear failure but understood it to be a part of the learning process. Profoundly, many students commented on the social responsibility they felt to engage the world in a meaningful way that makes the world a better place.[36]

Alice Berney outperformed all other schools in the Sacramento district on standard academic measures while offering students a much wider experience in the arts, culture, and hands-on projects such as gardening, sewing, and cooking.

The art of teaching in such a program involves observing what students can do and how they respond and then bringing them something new — a skill, a method, a concept, a story — at just the right time. We know when we have hit the mark by the degree of enthusiasm and determination as children take it up as their own. I can't imagine a more challenging and satisfying daily practice for a teacher.

The following memory predates my Waldorf experience but exemplifies how a subtle shift in focus from teacher-directed to student-inspired lessons can impact learning. I had chosen a Junior Great Books text for my second-grade language arts class because of the series' rich language and age-appropriate stories. The children enjoyed the tales, but they were most excited about learning new words that they could use in their own stories and conversations. We began a list on the blackboard of their favorite words from the stories. We titled the list "Words of Power." Soon the children began to add words that they had read or overheard, but not understood, from conversations at home. They did this spontaneously. It was not an assignment. We added these to our Words of Power, and the list grew, with words like soporific, synchronicity, catastrophe, surreptitious, and flabbergasted, to name just a few.

We tried to figure out the meanings of the words by how they were used in context. Sometimes, we acted them out. Sometimes, I read definitions from the dictionary to my students. The whole class was engaged and having fun using these words at home to impress their parents and to impress me in our discussions at school. Reading fluency was improving effortlessly.

We had exhausted our Junior Great Books by Easter, and I turned to an Open Court textbook series that the school had purchased. I was pleased that it presented classic stories and myths and planned to ignore the canned instructions to teachers, but after a few days, the children balked. They told me that they didn't like the new reader. When I asked them why, they conferred and quickly agreed that all the Words of Power had been taken out of the stories. Open Court had carefully limited the language to words that were prescribed for second graders. The children declared that these words were boring.

I asked them to tell me what made a word powerful, and they were quiet for a few minutes. Then Esme raised her hand and said, "When you look up a Word of Power in the dictionary and you read all the definitions, you still don't know everything it means." Moments such as this—when a child's eyes light up with enthusiasm and pride—were my reward.

If I had been teaching from prescribed standards, I would have introduced a vocabulary list and assigned the children to look up the words in the dictionary for homework. The final step would have been a spelling and definitions test. Most of the children would have dutifully accomplished the task and passed the test, but few, if any, would have adopted the words as their own and enjoyed using them. Some children would have struggled with the assignment and failed the test. Nothing in such an assignment would have led to Esme's insight about the limitations of dictionaries.

Trusting children meant paying close attention to how children responded to my lessons. Were they enthusiastically engaged, or were they going through the paces to please me or to get "a good grade"? This particular class was successful because I encouraged the children to bring their natural proclivities for learning language into the classroom. Our classroom, in turn, gave them an opportunity to expand their skills beyond what they could have accomplished on their own.

I was immersed in observing the children and following my sense of what worked best for them. In retrospect, I see that I was also learning to trust my instincts and intuition. At the time, I didn't step back from the process enough to label it. But I do remember a significant boost in my enthusiasm for teaching.

If teachers are focused only on a preset curriculum that they are charged to deliver, they may also miss the unusual gifts that some students carry. Isaac, a sixteen-year-old from South Philadelphia who used the subway to come downtown to our project at Friends Select School, was late one morning. He told me he had missed his subway stop. I asked if he had fallen asleep. He laughed and said, "No! I was playing a Bach fugue in my head, and I closed my eyes so I could hear the fourth voice. When it came in, I got lost in it and went right past my stop." I told him that was the best excuse I had ever heard! I was amazed by my son Paul's strong eidetic memory. Even as a young child, he could exactly reproduce drawings he had seen days or weeks before. He could start to draw at any point—the elephant's tusk or the whale's eye—because the whole drawing was so clear in his mind. His twin brother, Tim, was a kinesthetic learner who watched his father demonstrate how to ride a bike and then got on it and rode down the street with hardly a wobble. Did their teachers know this about them? And then there was sixth-grader Sara, who offered to explain Einstein's theory of relativity to our class when I confessed that I did not understand it well enough to teach it. Sara did, however, and she explained it at the board so simply and directly that even I could understand.

HOW TO HELP CHILDREN BECOME FLUENT
READERS AND WRITERS

1. **Trust children. Respect where they are developmentally.** Learning should be joyful, not stressful. Watch them carefully and protect them from undue anxiety and stress.

2. **Protect young children from premature academics.** The business of kindergarten is socialization and creative play. Academic instruction and worksheets create unnecessary stress that is damaging to young children. Children can learn instead to set the table for snacks and lunch, clean up after themselves, play games inside and outside, sing, and draw pictures. In the process, they learn to cooperate and follow directions.

3. **Consider starting children in first grade at age seven rather than six.** This would be helpful, particularly for young boys who are not ready to sit quietly at their desks, let alone start reading. Too many immature children are being diagnosed with ADD and medicated so that they can sit still for tasks they are not ready to perform.

4. **Take time introducing the alphabet and practicing the sounds the letters make.** Introduce simple words that start with each sound, and illustrate the word with a drawing. Some children may learn to read in the process. A child who enters first grade knowing how to read still profits from these developmentally appropriate exercises and lessons. Learning how to sound out words may help them rebalance their reading patterns to free up their right brains for imagining and understanding meaning. Use *Writing Road to Reading* as a resource in first and second grades to make sure that you have introduced all of the sounds.[37] Do you know how many different sounds "ough" makes?

5. **Provide daily physical exercises and activities that help children's brains integrate, mature, and become ready for academic challenges.** Teaching knitting to first graders, for example, is not a fuzzy extracurricular activity but a useful developmental tool. See Resources for particularly beneficial exercises.

6. **Bathe English-language learners in rich language.** Let them absorb, listen, and imitate without testing or pressure. Teachers should speak in a way that defines the words they are using. Find ways to check whether children understand without

putting them on the spot. Allow them to use their natural gift for learning language. Start teaching reading only when they are neurologically ready and have orally mastered basic English grammar and vocabulary.

7. **Watch for signs that a child may need special support.** One of my students kept missing the first sound of a word and often made mistakes in written math problems. A vision therapist discovered that letters and numbers were appearing and disappearing from his sight and was able, over time, to help him stabilize his focus. Another student, who resisted reading, told me that it gave him a headache after a few moments. The problem was solved by his reading specialist grandmother, who gave him an appropriately colored plastic sheet to put over the white paper.

8. **Give children opportunities to write and to practice making letters before they try to read.** When they are ready, writing their own sentences or stories is a sturdy bridge to reading.

9. **Substitute formative assessment (your written or spoken observation about how the child is doing) for grading, particularly in the lower grades.** Grading is harmful to children at both ends of the spectrum — those who struggle and those who are developmentally ahead of their classmates. Giving failing grades to children with developmental delays does not encourage them to work harder. It shuts them down.

For Parents: Read to your children. Read every day. Let your children pick out the books they want in the library and be prepared to read the ones they like multiple times. Don't stop reading at night when your children start school. Share books you have loved and discover new ones with them. Make reading together a precious, high-priority time. When your child starts to read, read together, take turns, and keep the process moving by filling in words when necessary. Don't push your child to read aloud if they don't want to do it. Trust them to let you know when they are ready.

. . . . .

Many children enter school with challenges that need to be worked with and overcome in a supportive, non-stressful environment. School programs that create stress and negative self-judgments compound problems. Teachers should not be required to stress and label young children. I believe in the resilience of children if they are given the love and recognition that they need, and I want to see teachers empowered and trained to be such agents.

Many of us carry wounds from educational experiences that have not trusted us, validated our efforts, or helped us overcome challenges. Those of us who become teachers and parents do not want to perpetuate harm. It is healing for teachers to be able to give children something we need but too often didn't receive — the trust that enables the children in our care to trust themselves and to fully develop all of their capacities. We want to promote healthy growth and the healing of our society by allowing ourselves and encouraging the children in our care to grow in creativity, curiosity, resilience, empathy, patience, competence, independence, and courage. And that is only the beginning of the list of possibilities when teachers and students forge strong relationships and begin to tell each other their stories.

Chapter Five

Tell Us a Story

Stories are compasses and architecture; we navigate by them; we build our sanctuaries and our prisons out of them and to be without a story is to be lost in the vastness of a world that spreads in all directions like arctic tundra or sea ice.

— Rebecca Solnit, *The Faraway Nearby*

Let me tell you a story. Yesterday, I struggled to put into words the importance of stories to learning. My mind was flooded with images: bright eyes all focused on me but seeing something beyond me — the troll, the princess, the youngest brother, the witch — responding to events as they unfolded — in the forest, in front of the castle, on the road. Once upon a time, and that time is always present as the children become joined with me, the storyteller, so the imagination can unfold. I see these same children as older children riding with Paul Revere and then crossing the Delaware with General Washington and his ragtag army. We could vividly imagine three hundred Spartans holding back the vast Persian army and allowing the Athenians to escape to the mountains so that the Golden Age of Athens could unfold, giving birth to philosophy, theater, science, and democracy. I can hear and see seventeen-year-old Julian speaking into the silence as we contemplated the closing verses of Dante's *Divine Comedy*, saying, "I knew that's what he would see!

He sees himself where he expected to see God! We are the end of the journey that we are on!"

Inspired by these memories, I wrote several pages about how we learn and how integral stories are to this process. I was sure that I saved it with a new title, *The Importance of Story*. But this morning, when I tried to open my document, my program told me that this document could not be restored, that it was gone, over, kaput. It was not in my files or the trash. Dear Readers, I know you are with me and can relate to what I am feeling because I have shared my story with you, and you have already made a connection to your own digital disasters. I am impelled, for your sakes as well as mine, to follow the path that thousands of good stories have taught me — to take a breath, let go of my losses, weep, if necessary, and begin again.

I wrote that good stories are as important for the growth of our minds and our souls as good food is for our bodies. This statement recognizes that stories, like food, can become toxic and make us ill, can poison our minds with lies as well as nurture their growth. If I tell a false story about you and get you in trouble, I can break more than the truth. I can break our friendship. I can break your heart. The quality of our lives depends on the quality of the stories we tell ourselves and each other, particularly the stories that we tell our children.

I remember Beau Bergdahl, a young man who dominated the news for a few weeks. He wrote home from the war in Afghanistan that he felt betrayed because the story he had been told about how he would help the Afghan people was not the story that he was having to live out. When we are betrayed by a story we were willing to risk our lives for, we are set adrift and lose our coordinates. We become lost.

When citizens believe lies promoted by self-serving leaders, our democracy is threatened, and our body politic divides. How has our education system predisposed us to believe such lies?

Rebecca Solnit tells us how essential stories are to learning. She tells us stories are much more than entertainment; they are compasses, orienting us to the world.

Fairytales are about trouble, about getting into and out of it and trouble seems to be a necessary stage on the route of becoming. All the magic and glass mountains and plants the size of houses and princesses beautiful as the day and talking birds and part-time serpents are distractions from the tough core of most stories — the struggle to survive against adversaries, to find your place in the world and to come into your own. Difficulty is always a school, though learning is optional.[38]

Neuroscience can now demonstrate how stories activate the brain. Broca's area, the language-processing part of our brains, is activated when we listen to a PowerPoint presentation or a lecture filled with facts. But our brains begin to twinkle like Christmas trees when we are told a story. Sensory details awaken the sensory cortex; action stimulates the motor cortex, and so on. The brains of the listeners synchronize with the brain of the storyteller.

I was not surprised to learn this because, as a storyteller and actress, I know when the audience is with me. I know when I don't have their full attention, and I know what I have to do to get it. I have to turn on sensory, motor, and emotional centers in my brain. I have to see, smell, hear, feel what I am describing, and then the audience will, too, invariably because this is how we are wired. If I can make children laugh, weep, or both, they may remember not only the events of the story but the feeling and the meaning behind it. If this experience speaks to their own questions, the story may become a guide for their lives.

Kieran Egan, education professor at Simon Frazier University and author of *Memory, Imagination and Learning: Connected by Story,* describes how imagination develops out of our need to remember and share information:

Imagination is not some desirable but dispensable frill, but... it is the heart of any truly educational experience; it is not something split off from "the basics" or disciplined thought or rational inquiry, but is the quality that can give them life and meaning; it is not something belonging properly to the arts, but is central to all areas of the curriculum; it is not something to ornament our recreational hours, but is the hard pragmatic center of all effective human thinking... Stimulating the imagination is not an alternative educational activity to be argued for in competition with other claims; it is a prerequisite to making any activity educational (Egan and Nadaner, 1988, p. ix). One result of using such an approach is to see lessons and units as good stories to be told rather than as sets of objectives to be attained. [39]

In my classrooms, it was stories all the way, up and down, from first grade through high school. I told stories to introduce curriculum, to stimulate imagination and memory, and to teach new skills. My courses were most effective when they were organized and presented within the framework of an ongoing story rather than as a series of facts and procedures.

Forming a class or a group of young students is a challenging task. One of my colleagues described it as "herding cats." To support this process, I told my first graders about a group of children who lived in a castle in a valley kingdom. An enemy threatened their kingdom, and their parents decided to send the children into the mountains to safety until the conflict was over. The children were led on this journey by a trusted teacher, who brought along his dog and a donkey to carry food and provisions. Each day presented the children with new obstacles—crossing a rushing stream, walking along a narrow mountain path, meeting wild animals—and the children learned each day that they could all survive only by helping each other. The children in the class recognized themselves and each other in the story children that I described for them.

At night, around the fire, the teacher told his children (and mine) a story to bring them comfort from their fears and courage for the challenges ahead. This nest of stories lasted for weeks until it was time for winter break. Word came to the children that it was safe to return home. The story children who came down from the mountains were very changed from the children who had gone up, just as my class had begun to change from a group of competitive individuals into a more harmonious chorus. I did not have to give them boring lectures about cooperation or why they should wait their turn. They were working instead with the images and events I had imagined and described for them, joyfully imitating and enthusiastically helping each other mature and learn.

This was a much more effective way to facilitate social growth than using a pre-boxed lesson plan or "bullying program." I realize, looking back, how transformative this experience was. Years of experience and insight poured into this opportunity to tell a story that would connect me with my first graders and let them know my intentions. Our story built trust between us and sparked their desire to write stories, too.

One of my most challenging tasks as a teacher without textbooks was to find the story that would capture the essence of the moment: a breakthrough scientific discovery, a turning point in history, or an important debate. To introduce a chemistry unit on combustion, I told seventh graders the story of a young French nobleman named Antoine Lavoisier, who was passionately interested in a new science called "chemistry." Lavoisier created a chemistry laboratory that attracted young scientists from all over the world, including Ben Franklin and James Watt. Lavoisier's team burned different objects outside and inside of air-tight containers and discovered that an element of "air" combined with other elements to form compounds when set ablaze. Lavoisier named this element "oxygen." His experiments demonstrated that oxygen combines with hydrogen to form water. The ancient Greeks had believed that air and water were elements — basic substances — so this new finding contradicted all accepted theories. Lavoisier's combustion experiments established the first basic law of chemistry — that matter cannot be created or destroyed, that it can only be transformed into new compounds of mixed elements. His revolutionary discoveries occurred during a time of intense political and social revolution in France. Even though he was known for supporting initiatives that improved the lives of ordinary citizens, the Revolutionary Tribunal arrested Lavoisier and tried and beheaded him on what were later acknowledged to be false charges. We revisited his story when we studied the French Revolution the following year.

We had just started an eighth-grade unit about weather, and I wanted the children to have a graphic understanding of the narrow band of atmosphere in which life is possible. I told them the story of James Glaisher, founder of the British Meteorological Society, and Henry Coxwell, an experienced balloonist, who took a cage of pigeons up in a balloon in 1862. They intended to measure temperature, pressure, and humidity and their effects on animals. The balloon was launched into the clutches of a rising storm and went up through lightning and thunder. At 16,500 feet, they tossed a pigeon over the basket and watched it flutter chaotically down toward earth. At twenty-three thousand feet, they tossed out another one, which plummeted out of view before gaining some flight ability. At twenty-six thousand feet, the last two pigeons refused to leave the cage. The men noticed that the release cord for the gas valve that would allow them to descend was tangled out of reach. They were still rising. At thirty thousand feet, Glaisher started to lose consciousness, and Coxwell climbed the rigging to untangle the cord. His fingers froze to the metal structure, so he caught the cord with his teeth and tugged it, first breaking a tooth and then tearing through the flesh of his cheek. The third time, he bit the cord hard and jumped, tearing the skin from the hand, which was frozen to the metal valve. He landed in the gondola basket. They had reached nearly thirty-six thousand feet, the limit of human survival, before they began their descent.

Stories are not only a powerful way to introduce a subject; they can also be an effective way for students to demonstrate what they have learned. In fourth grade, after investigating the rock cycle for their first course in geology, my students completed the following assignment:

> *Today, you will interview a rock and write its life story. Select one of the rocks you have met or are interested in. Put the rock*

in front of you. Begin the interview. (The rock is telepathic and can hear your silent questions. You must listen very carefully to hear what the rock has to say.)

Ask it, "Where were you found?" "How did you get there?" "What were you like before you became the rock you are now?" "What was it like when you took your present form?" "Where did you come from before that?" "And before that?" "Where were you first born?" "What was it like then?" And any other question you think is important. When you finish, draw a picture about the story of the rock; it could be from an interesting event in its life, or it could show several stages in its life, as in a cartoon.

Here are some lines from the stories that the students wrote in response:

- "For millions of years I tumbled on the ocean bottom, tossing and turning."

- "I was born with the earth and have no further memory of time before that."

- "It was very strange changing from a very hot orange liquid to the cold silver and greyish white color I am now."

- "About 1,000 years went by and the oceans sank away and I was left on a mountain."

- "I came from a place beyond the end of the universe, a place of beauty and light, a place where all matter will go some time, a place of rest, beyond all reach, in the unending fields of oblivion."

If you only ask children for the right answers to set questions, you will miss such surprises. Tragically, so will they. When children use their imaginations to create stories, they form lasting memories to hold the information they have learned.

So, how is it that our schools have wandered far from the source — the wellspring of stories — within our culture and our imaginations? We know that a primary ingredient for future academic success is the number and quality of stories read or told to young children. The second ingredient is how much they, in turn, read and write their own stories. Children who have been steeped in good literature not only have broader vocabularies, but their brains are more active, and they are able to make more meaningful connections among experiences and ideas. Such children are more curious and open to reading for information because the information connects to their questions and helps them understand and flesh out the stories that inspire them.

This process can be deadened by reading comprehension questions and analysis. When you ask pre-adolescent children why they like a story, they will most likely start to tell you the story rather than talk about it. This tells the teacher that they are living it over in their imaginations and are not yet able to step outside of their experience and look back at it objectively. Instead, they are doing an essential practice that builds strong memory capacities. Why have we allowed textbook and test publishers, who are not informed about child development and have never taught children, to tell us what the children should know and be able to do at a given age?

Looking at the reading comprehension questions on the STAR test or in the Common Core, which are supposed to objectively measure reading competency, I am reminded of a conversation with my youngest son. His excellent fifth-grade teacher had to take a leave of absence, and substitute teachers filled her position. I had been my son's language arts teacher in the fourth grade, and I knew that he tested and performed far above his grade level. His report card, however, showed that he had an "F" in reading. "How did you manage to do that?" I asked him.

"Easy," he answered. "Read from page thirty-two to thirty-eight and then answer the questions on pages thirty-nine to forty-three."

"You didn't answer the questions," I said.

He told me I was right and that he didn't do it because the questions were stupid. And then he said, "You know, Miss — doesn't know who I am. She doesn't see me at all. I don't care if she gives me an 'F.'"

Even if Kelsey had answered the multiple-choice questions, the teacher would have known very little about him, his capacities, or his questions. An "A" would have been equally meaningless.

Stories that guide and direct us are handed down through relationship, often by a parent or teacher but sometimes by an author the child turns to again and again as a trusted friend, as one who speaks truth to some deep question or concern. Finding just the right story to tell or read to a group of children is a wonderful feeling.

I am reminded of an experience I had many years ago. I had taken a break from full-time teaching to spend more time with my young sons. I signed up as a substitute in the Oakland Unified School District. I was called to teach in a high school in East Oakland. It was a locked-down campus, serving primarily African American students. It would be described now as a "failing" school. I was told where to go but given no instructions or attendance rolls.

The classroom was only half full when I arrived. I had come prepared, however, and after introducing myself, I asked the students if they would like me to read them a story. They shrugged and nodded as I began to read them *The Bear* by William Faulkner. I was surprised to notice that as the story progressed, the room was slowly filling with students. Even the young man by the window, who had been nodding out at the beginning of the period, was listening intently. At the end of the period, I asked them what they thought about the story, and they were responsive. Then I asked them if their English teacher read them stories, and they told me, "No! No one ever does that!" I read stories to full classes for the rest of the day. At the end of the day, the woman in the office was surprised to see me. She said, "You survived! Not many substitutes do that."

The more money that is cut from the schools, the more standards that are prescribed, the more tests there are that cause children to flail and fail, the less time teachers have to do the real work: helping to remove impediments, both physical and emotional, that are in the way of each child's full flowering. This flowering has nothing to do with the number of computers in the classroom or the ratio of nonfiction to fiction assigned, but it does have to do with the teacher's ability to see each child, discern what is needed, and find the right medicine, often embedded in just the right story. Direct criticism and correction can increase anxiety and weaken attachment, especially for young children, effectively shutting down their learning potential. A story, however, allows a child to safely imagine and experience new paths of action.

Here is a story I wrote for a particularly dreamy first grader but told to all the children:

THE PROUD PRINCE

Not so far away or so long ago, a young boy named Sam lived happily with his mother, his dog, Rufus, and his wide imagination. Now, Sam was a fine young lad, good at games, kind to his friends, and thoughtful of his dear mother. He loved the plants and flowers that grew all about his small village, and there was nothing he liked better than to play outside in all weather.

Whether he played alone or with friends, he could always imagine a wonderful game. Sometimes, he was a pirate sailing over a sea of grass in his wheelbarrow boat; sometimes, he was an explorer searching for rare beasts in the woods next to his house. Sam's only serious fault, if you could call it that, was that he got so involved in his games that he didn't hear his mother calling, forgot to take the garbage out, and sometimes left his jacket or shoes in strange places, never to be seen again.

It was not easy for Sam's understanding mother to get her dreamy son to school on time, and once at school, Miss Bailey was not always as understanding and patient as Sam's mother. "Sam, Sam, where are you now?" Miss Bailey would say. "Be with us, and please pay attention, or you will never learn to read, write, and solve math problems."

This day, Sam was trying his best to pay attention as Miss Bailey told an interesting story. It was about a young prince who wasn't afraid of anything and who had decided to leave his father's house to seek his fortune. Sam imagined him riding down the road from the castle on his beautiful black pony into a forest glade. Miss Bailey's voice faded away, and there was Sam, the young knight, leading his horse up to the edge of a beautiful lake to drink. The water looked so inviting that Sam thought he might take a little swim, which he did until he was tired, and then what better than a little nap under the tree where he had tied his horse? He was just having a lovely dream when Miss Bailey's voice woke him with a start. "Sam!" she said. "Could you tell the class about the Proud Prince's first adventure?"

"Well," said Sam, "he rode out of the castle, and it was such a fine day that he took a shortcut through the woods, where he found a beautiful lake where he had a swim and then took a lovely nap in which he dreamed about having an adventure with a giant."
Sam's voice got softer and softer as Miss Bailey's frown got bigger and bigger.

The other children didn't laugh because they really liked Sam and were embarrassed for him. But Miss Bailey said, "Sam, see me at recess," which was the worst thing of all because Sam truly loved recess and was looking forward to playing an exciting game of kickball with his friends.

At recess, Miss Bailey talked very seriously to Sam, and he decided that he would try his best to pay attention all the rest of the day. But this was a hard day for Sam to pay attention. Tomorrow was his birthday, and he was very excited about all the wonderful gifts his mother might be planning for him. More than anything, Sam wanted to be like that young prince, riding his fine horse, dressed in fine clothes, and while Miss Bailey taught the class their reading lesson, Sam dreamed about his birthday gifts, his party, and his cake. Before he knew it, school was over, and he was ready to go home without learning how to read even one new word.

Sam ran home as fast as he could. But his loving mother was not at the door to greet him with a hug and a kiss as usual. He went inside to find her sitting in a chair with her foot propped up on a stool and bandages all around her ankle. "Oh, Sam, dear, I am so sorry. I tripped and fell this morning and twisted my ankle, and the doctor says that I have to stay off my feet for a few days. I haven't been able to go to the market to get your birthday presents, but, my dear, I have made a list." She showed the list to Sam and asked him if he could read it.

Sam said, "Sure I can!" and put it quickly in his pocket without looking very closely. And, indeed, Sam was so excited that he was sure he could read, and he imagined himself already in the market, buying his gifts. So, he didn't hear all of his mother's careful instructions on where to go and who to see, just the end, which was to be home in time for supper, which Sam's neighbor was bringing over to help his mother. Then he put the money his mother gave him into a little pouch and put it on top of his note, holding it in his pocket so he wouldn't lose it.

He felt so grown up that he didn't even imagine himself doing anything but running as fast as he could to the big marketplace in the center of town.

When Sam got there, he took out his note and tried to read it. The first words on the list said, "A GOLD COAT." Sam knew the first word. That's an A, he thought. But he didn't know the second letter or the sound it made. Surely, it didn't make that much difference. He would just forget it and use the next three letters, which he could remember. "O L D—OLD," said Sam. Now, what was the sound for the letter C? Sam wrinkled his eyes and ears, trying to remember, and came out with a G. That was it! An OLD GOAT. What could his mother possibly want with an old goat? And where would he find one?

He thought maybe the next words on the list might be easier. "A BLACK FOAL." Well, he knew A, and he knew B and K, and he thought that the second letter was L. Carefully sounding out the word, Sam read, "Black." Black what? He did not know the first letter of the last word. What was black that ended in O A L? "COAL," said Sam. "Black coal is what my mother wants."

Now for the third item, "CAKE and CANDLES." Now we already know that Sam had trouble with the letter C. He tried again, and this time, he made a sound like the letter S. He forgot, though, about the silent E making the A say its own name, so this is what he read: "SACK and SANDALS." His mother must want sandals to wear for her hurt foot.

Sam found the man who made sandals, and he bought a pair and put them in a sack. An old woman sold him pieces of black coal for the stove. And Sam finally found a farmer who had goats for sale. Sam bought the oldest one and tied a rope around his neck. But he was late for supper because the goat had a mind of its own and had to stop to eat grass, bushes, and anything else in its path all the way to Sam's house.

A disappointed but dutiful Sam finally tied the goat to the fence and went in to give the coal and the sandals to his dear mother, who was beginning to worry about him. "Oh, Sam, Sam," his mother said. "Do you still have the note, dear?" Sam nodded and gave it all crumpled to her. She smoothed it out and asked him to sit beside her, and together, they read the words:

"A GOLD COAT—I had it made for you at the tailor's," said his mother. "A BLACK FOAL—Farmer Jones has a beautiful colt. It will be yours as soon as it is old enough to leave its mother. I wanted you to see it. CAKE and CANDLES—The baker, Sam, has your special birthday cake." Sam looked at his mother, and his mother looked at him and said, "Did you really buy an old goat?" And Sam said, "Yes!" and they both began to laugh, and the goat laughed, too, sticking his head in the window.

The next day, Miss Bailey noticed a big change in Sam. When it came time for reading, his eyes were bright and looking at the board, and when she asked him a question, Sam knew the answer because he had been listening very carefully. "Whatever has gotten into you, Sam?" she said. "Maybe it's your birthday."

And from then on, Sam saved his wonderful imagination for recesses, long summer days, weekends, and reading. Because now that Sam could read, a whole new world of imagination opened up to him. And Miss Bailey only occasionally had to say, "Sam, pay attention," and then they would both smile.

The quality of our civic life depends on the quality of the stories we tell ourselves about who we are and what we can expect from the world around us. Learning to ask, "Is that story true?" must become a reflexive response if we aspire to be both free and fully human, able to know and express ourselves as well as empathize and act for the good of others. Learning to differentiate between fiction and fact is a critical study, particularly for older students.

High school students should be made conscious that we think in stories rather than in facts. We tell stories to ourselves to make sense of our experiences and to unify our common life. Different groups of people, over time, have told themselves many different stories about the nature of reality and why they should choose one path of action rather than another.

In elementary school, we can note this fact as we study different cultures and mythologies and begin to think about the reasons for these differences. In high school, history and science should be studied through this lens, and students can begin to investigate the consequences of confusing fiction with facts or partial facts with systemic reality. They need to be clear about the difference between fact and fiction. We can change and adapt our stories to meet changing conditions, but we can't change the fact that increasing carbon emissions increases catastrophic changes in the earth's climate. Describing immigrants at our borders as hordes of criminals who are threatening our safety and security is a story, albeit a false one, that has consequences. Understanding that farm families leaving Honduras are suffering from climate-related drought and famine is another story based on fact. As the mega-stories devised to support our modern neo-liberal systems continue to falter, the next generation will be tasked with creating stories that support a global society capable of realizing the goals of sustainability and well-being for all people.

HOW TO BECOME A STORYTELLER

I share stories of my experiences as a teacher because these stories hold the memories that are the core of what I learned from the children and want to communicate. My commentaries and explanations are secondary and reflective. I believe that it is the stories that will stay with you and inspire you to try the following suggestions.

1. **Practice telling stories.** If teachers do not receive this support from their credential programs, they can practice in faculty workshops or in-service training. Tell stories "by heart" whenever possible. Telling a story is generally more effective than reading stories out loud. I often taped the stories that I wanted to tell and listened to them at night or as I commuted to school in the morning.

2. **Practice activating your imagination and sensory centers and create vivid pictures of events, places, and characters.** Teachers can tell by the looks on students' faces whether their reading or telling is bringing a story to life.

3. **Tell students your stories.** This sharing will deepen your connection with them. If your tale describes something you learned the hard way or from hearing or reading a story, so much the better. I encouraged students and parents to tell their stories throughout our eight years together. In first grade, parents told the story of their child's birth during the birthday celebration. In third grade, parents told stories of how their child's ancestors came to the United States, again during their birthday celebrations. At the end of the year, I collected these stories and made a booklet for each child called *Ancestor Stories*.

4. **Use stories to introduce concepts.** I introduced my second graders to systems ecology by writing a series of interconnected stories titled *Mother Oak*. Each story described one of the creatures whose lives were intertwined with and dependent on a large oak tree. The stories also traced the fates of a small group of acorns that is shaken from a limb during a thunderstorm. Research Gate offers guidance on how to frame your lessons or unit of study as a story.[40]

5. **Write pedagogical stories that address particular students or issues facing a class.** Pedagogical stories are written to instruct and heal as well as to amuse or inspire students. There are websites with examples of such stories,[41] but the best and most successful stories are the ones that each teacher crafts with a

particular students in mind. These stories are told to the whole class so that students can internalize the message without feeling singled out or embarrassed. A self-aware child may recognize and appreciate that the story is a gift written just for them.

6. **Help students discern true stories based on fact or thoughtful inquiry from "fake news" stories designed to manipulate their emotions.** We swim in a sea of manipulative stories, from advertising to political agendas that create longing, fear, and division. Train students to ask, "Is this true?" to investigate, and to be open to considering alternative points of view before repeating or believing any story.

7. **Involve students in collecting and presenting stories from their communities.** This can be done as dramatic presentations or as podcasts modeled on Story Corps.

8. **Use every opportunity to tell children a new story of our place within the natural world.** Economist and philosopher Charles Eisenstein calls for an overarching narrative that views the earth not as a dead rock with resources to exploit but as a living system whose health depends on the health of its organs and tissues — its wetlands, forests, seagrass, mangroves, fish, corals, and more.[42]

For Parents: Tell your children stories from your life. Make up stories for them. The stories you create for your child can be great teaching tools, much more effective than parental lectures. Share stories that were important for your growth and development. As always, read to your children, and as they mature, discuss what you have read together.

· · · · ·

We are faced with daunting challenges in our time. Sharing our stories reassures us that we are not alone, that others have coped with difficult situations, solved difficult problems, and found the strength to learn and grow through experience. Such stories inspire children to try out new ideas as they bring stories to life through purposeful play. Purposeful play, Abraham Maslow tells us, is the basis for all creativity and the arts.

Chapter Six

Let Them Play

The creation of something new is not accomplished by the intellect, but by the play instinct acting from inner necessity. The creative mind plays with objects it loves.

—Carl Jung

If relationship is the crucible for learning, play is the catalyst. Carl Jung tells us that play is not an option but a basic instinct, fundamentally connected to learning and survival. Young children play with their food, with their tasks, with their sounds. Any interesting object becomes a toy. They dawdle on the path, distracted by the life around them, living in the present moment in sharp contrast to their goal-driven and time-ridden parents, who must hurry them along to get somewhere. They also make incredible strides in learning in a very short time.

As children mature into adolescence, the pull of play continues to be strong. It is a force that animates their school years, as young students resist the division between work and play that teachers are charged to enforce. It is a force that can reignite in graduate schools and start-up enterprises when students and former students finally get to follow their own questions, interests, and creative proclivities.

The primacy of instinctual play behavior holds true for the entire animal kingdom. Research even suggests that animals who play the most are the ones that survive best. In his book *Play,*

Stuart Brown tells us, "Play fighting may let a bear learn when it can trust another bear and, if things get too violent, when it needs to defend itself or flee. Play allows 'pretend' rehearsal for the challenges and ambiguities of life, a rehearsal in which life and death are not at stake."[43] Neuroscientists in Canada and Australia collaborated on a study that tabulated play in fifteen species of mammals, from dogs to dolphins. They found a direct correlation between the amount of play and brain size. Additional research pinpoints that the period of play in each species is tied to the development of the brain's frontal cortex, the region most responsible for cognition and the rate and growth of the cerebellum, now thought to be responsible for important cognitive functions such as attention and language processing.[44] Our propensity for play may be the primary reason that humans have been successful as a species.

Stuart Brown confirms everything I've learned about play from observing, teaching, and parenting children — that play is a primary need, not an optional activity, essential to the development of social skills, adaptability, intelligence, creativity, problem solving, and more. Dr. Brown is a psychiatrist, clinical researcher, founder of the National Institute for Play, producer of a three-part PBS series, and regular consultant to Fortune 500 companies and groups. He offers ample support for his understanding that play is as important to our health and well-being as sleep and nutrition and may be a determining factor in our adult success and happiness.

> *Play's process of capturing a pretend narrative and combining it with the reality of one's experience in a playful setting is, at least in childhood, how we develop our major personal understanding of how the world works. We do so initially by imagining possibilities — simulating what might be, and then testing this against what actually is.*
>
> *Though this may seem to be a primarily childish trait, close examination of adult internal narratives (our stream of consciousness) reveals something similar… We daydream about events in our future. These thoughts leave an imprint on*

our brains that constructs imaginative new combinations. And in creating those novel combinations, we find what works... In playing we foster the creation of new circuits and test them by running signals through them. Because play is a non-essential activity, this testing is done safely, when survival (or success) is not at stake.[45]

Play is the warp that all the chapters of this book weave through. Children happily play games of various sorts, play music, act in plays, make up stories, use the natural world as a playground, play around with tools, with technology, with ideas, with artistic media, to mention only a few possibilities. In the process, they develop multiple capacities that allow them to become successful adults, capable of creating something new. Even in the so-called work world, the most successful scientists, engineers, artists, and entrepreneurs are arguably adults who "love their work" because they approach it with a playful frame of mind.

Jung tells us that the creative mind plays with objects it loves. If our work allows and challenges us to be present, to be resourceful, to trust our intuitions, to use our creativity, to play with ideas and objects that are stimulating, it can be deeply satisfying, and we may rightly say that we love our work. However strenuous and demanding, it will never be deadening. I loved teaching; it was never boring, always full of challenges and an opportunity to learn and grow. Scripted lessons and textbooks are anathema to this enjoyment. I am like the children. When I am told what I have to do and say by an outside authority, something that could be joyful quickly becomes drudgery.

If we accept that play is the primary instinct by which children learn and develop capacities, then our schools must provide ample time and support for child-directed free play, particularly in the lower grades. Playful approaches to academic learning will always be more successful than didactic directives up and down the grades.

I learned about futility trying to teach eighth graders English grammar from a textbook. I much more effectively taught basic grammar to my third-grade class by staging a playful grammar drama. My students were familiar with the creation story of Adam and Eve. The cast was Adam, two describing angels, a scribe, and a large, unruly group of animals. I played God. Two words were written on the blackboard above Adam's head: "NOUN" and "VERB." Each angel held a sign: "ADJECTIVE" or "ADVERB." The animals decided who they were and, one by one, hopped, flapped, slithered, or crept to the center of the room. Adam gave them their names after watching them move. When the animal felt suitably named, God added an action—the eagle swooped. Then the describing angels added their words—the powerful eagle swooped down. The scribe wrote this sentence in his book. Everyone got a chance to be Adam, an angel, God, and the scribe. By the time we finished, we had practiced the exercise dozens of times, and the children wanted to do more.

During a follow-up exercise, I told the children that every day they create new sentences, some that may never have been uttered before. They loved this idea. So, I went through the class, assigning each of them a part of speech following a simple sentence pattern: Article Adjective Noun Verb Adverb Preposition Noun. Each child wrote down their word secretly, and then we put the words together. Many sentences were nonsense, but a few were definite originals. The children took those sentences, drew pictures of them, and put them up around the room. My favorite (and I actually remember it!) was "The silly pope hopped crazily on Jupiter." The accompanying irreverent drawing of an old man with a pointed hat and his tongue hanging out, holding up his robes and hopping on a rather small facsimile of Jupiter, made us all laugh. We had fun doing this, and the results were comparatively fantastic when it came to learning parts of speech.

Experiences that engage us, that go in deep enough to make us laugh or cry, stay with us throughout life and are easy to recall in detail. I have found this to be consistently true as I have mined my memories in the process of writing this book.

As part of their graduation ceremony, my students also recounted memorable moments. Clayton shared the following:

In 7th grade we were studying the art of writing about emotions. It had been a normal recess until Ms. C came up to me and asked if I could do her a favor. Seeing as I am such a good person, I said, "Yes." But what she said next shocked me. She asked me to do something no single student had ever done before. The next day, I made room in my desk and had "it" ready. Main lesson began again as usual, but Ms. C soon asked me to take off my hat. I refused. We had a loud argument about it, and then I did it. I reached in my desk, pulled out my carefully made shaving cream pie, and put it RIGHT in her face!! Then she retaliated with a seemingly bigger pie, and I was shocked as much as my classmates. We then had to write about what we felt when I pied Ms. C... but who cares... I got to pie Ms. C!!!!

At Summerfield Waldorf High School, I taught quarter-long writing classes through the grades. Ninth graders produced an autobiography of their childhood memories with a focus on sentence and paragraph structure. Tenth graders learned how to write inductive essays, examining evidence and multiple points of view before arriving at a conclusion or leaving the conclusion up to the reader. Juniors were encouraged to breathe out and playfully explore language, images, and ideas in creative writing, and seniors learned how to research and write term papers. All forms of writing can arguably be creative, and the difference in the junior writing course was primarily one of approach. Here is my overview for the course, taking inspiration from Paul Matthews's *Sing Me the Creation* — a sourcebook for poets, teachers, and all who wish to develop the life of the imagination.[46]

GENERAL INSTRUCTIONS

1. **Buy a spiral notebook or a small loose-leaf binder.** Keep this notebook only for this class. Write in it daily (at least 20 minutes), doing assignments or free writing. At the end of the quarter,

the number of pages will be counted (assuming 250 words per page). The number of pages required for an "A" grade will be determined by the end of the second week of class. I will not grade the exercises or your creative pieces.

2. **RULES**
    a. You may break the rules of any exercise if the spirit moves you.

    b. You may collaborate with your classmates.

    c. You may use ideas or phrases from your classmates or other writers.

    d. You may be as silly as you please.

    e. You may speak to whomever or whatever you care to (from worms to God).

    f. You may lie and exaggerate.

    g. You may begin in the middle and stop before the end.

    h. It's OK to enjoy yourself in the process.

    i. You do not have to be PC.

Thursday, April 18, Exercise Four: Write an "I remember" piece — either random impressions or one leading to another. They do not have to be deep confessions about your life. The aim is to give vivid details, including the names of people. There is no need to interpret, philosophize, or be sequential. (I did all exercises with my students and shared my writing as an equal rather than a model.)

I remember the first snow, running outside in the crisp morning, falling flat on my back and moving my arms and legs up and down and in and out to make an angel shape, the taste of fresh snow on my tongue. I remember the night my daddy came back from Kwajalein, how he hitchhiked most of the night instead of waiting for the bus, how he held me tightly in his arms, strange after two years gone in the war. I remember my great-grandmother Christine, sitting in the rocking chair by the heater, combing and braiding her long gray hair in the morning light. I remember wearing pink socks and black suede shoes and dancing to "Rock Around the Clock" with Duane. I remember them holding Kelsey up so I could see him and touching my index finger to his. "Hello!" I remember the moon shining on the ocean and the fire reflecting in Dale's face, how we held each other that night on the beach. I remember Follow's eyes looking up into mine with infinite sadness and resignation when we left her at the veterinary hospital at UC Davis. I remember sleeping in the old camping trailer on an iron double bed, first with my father and mother and Linda and David and later with John and Timmy and Paul and Kelsey, a safe little world inside wild or strange surroundings. I remember a student rushing into the door while my class was reading the assassination scene from Julius Caesar, shouting, "The President has been shot! The President has been shot!" (A.C.)

At the end of one such class, Luke told me that he finally felt like he knew how to write, that he had something to say that others might enjoy and that he was looking forward to doing more writing now that he didn't dread it.

Playful approaches to learning work well because they stimulate students' natural learning proclivities. Observation and brain science also indicate that physical movement is key to creating new neural pathways, healing disabilities as well as supporting healthy development. Hopping, jumping, throwing, skipping, and clapping games are essential adjuncts to classroom learning. Children have always known that their activities at recess are important, and adults can learn from watching what students do when they are not adult directed.

My high school students would stand outside between classes and during breaks, kicking a hacky sack around, alone or in groups. My middle school students liked to juggle and take on balance challenges like the unicycle.

An elementary school in Texas that decided to follow the Finnish education model and expand recess to one hour from twenty minutes a day reported that after a few months, the children were less distracted in class, made more eye contact, tattled less, and had moved considerably ahead of schedule academically.[47]

Dr. David Katz, director of Yale School of Medicine's Prevention Research Center, supports this perspective in a recent article titled "Ritalin or Recess?"

> *Children used to play outside. They used to have Physical Education and recess during the school day. More and more we take naturally rambunctious children, send them to schools from which recess and Physical Education have been all but banished, bolt them to chairs all day long, and then watch them grow into adults that can't get off their couches with crowbars. And, alas, along the way we medicate more and more of them for attention disorders. Could it be that WE are the ones who have not been paying sufficient attention to the natural healthy restlessness of children?[48]*

As schools limit or eliminate recess and physical activities, they are experiencing an alarming leap in the number of children diagnosed with ADD or ADHD. In the eight years between 2003 and 2011, the number of children diagnosed with ADHD grew by two million, with one million more children prescribed medication (usually Ritalin or Adderall). This adds up to 11 percent of children overall, including one in five high school boys — with over 6 percent of all children on medication, including ten thousand toddlers.[49]

What is going on here? The ruling assumption is that attention deficit is an inherited genetic defect that can be treated most effectively through medication. However, diagnosis and treatment based on anecdotal information and observation vary widely from state to state and radically from country to country. Learning specialists rechecking children diagnosed with ADHD and taking medication in South Carolina found that only 39.5 percent of the children retested met the definition.[50] In comparison to the 6 percent of American children who were taking medication for ADD or ADHD in 2011, less than 0.5 percent of French and Italian school-age children were diagnosed and medicated for hyperactivity.[51]

Medicating for attention deficit is a cash cow for pharmaceutical companies. A 2013 *New York Times* editorial questioned misleading advertising by drug companies as well as soaring profits on stimulants sold to both children and adults:

> *The F.D.A. has cited every major A.D.H.D. drug, including the stimulants Adderall, Concerta, Focalin and Vyvanse, for false and misleading advertising since 2000, some of them multiple times. The companies, when challenged, typically stop those misleading claims, but the overall impact appears marginal. The number of prescriptions for A.D.H.D. drugs for adults ages 20 to 39 nearly tripled between 2007 and 2012, and sales of stimulant medications in 2012 were more than five times higher than a decade earlier.* [52]

While there may be short-term benefits in prescribing stimulants to improve school performance, there are also many unanswered questions about their addictiveness as well as long-term effects on brain development, capacities, and overall health.

Dr. Gabor Maté, co-author of *Hold On to Your Kids* and author of *Scattered: How Attention Deficit Disorder Originates and What You Can Do About It*, holds an alternate view that attention deficit and hyperactivity are reversible developmental delays with origins in infancy rather than genetically inherited diseases. He thinks that the best way to increase dopamine, the brain chemical that is deficient in children experiencing attention challenges, is through nurturing interaction with attentive, attached adults:

> *Not everyone's brains work the same way. It is folly to impose uniform expectations as if there were no differences in brain chemistry, emotional needs, or maturational levels from one child to the next. There has to be enough flexibility in the system to allow for individual thought patterns and learning styles.*
>
> *In these days of cash-register approaches to education among the first to be sacrificed have been learning assistants and teachers' aides — the very people who could give classroom teachers some*

respite and offer the many needy students in our schools patient tutoring, individual contact, and emotional support. The most troubled of these children are increasingly lost, desperate, angry, and, sooner or later, almost beyond help. If such policies continue, the cost to society will be enormous, to the children devastating... Blaming a child for his restlessness and trying to control it with punishment or coercion will not work. In the short term, he may be helped by medication, but the long-term question is how to enable him to develop so that he can acquire some psychological rest and impulse control. Schools cannot on their own meet these highly sensitive children's hunger for attention, love, and acceptance, but they can begin by not making the problem worse through ill-conceived disciplinary measures.[53]

Over the eight years that I had the privilege of observing my students, I repeatedly noted that students with challenges were drawn to particular physical activities and that they were able to significantly improve or overcome these challenges on their own.

Theron was born prematurely and survived only because he was an unusually strong infant. As is the case with most preemies, he experienced some developmental delays. As a young child, his lungs were not fully developed, making him prone to infection. He eventually accomplished all benchmarks, physical and academic, but with greater effort than some of his peers. His parents' loving support, coupled with his strong basic intelligence, suggested that he only needed time to fully integrate and catch up.

As the years passed, he needed less and less special attention. He made noticeable strides when he became a skilled unicyclist. By seventh grade, the only signs I could see of his developmental challenges were slight breaks in the letter formation of his handwriting. As he learned to balance and perform with the diabolo in his eighth-grade year, these breaks disappeared, and by graduation, he was excelling in all areas. Theron described his experience with the diabolo at his graduation ceremony.

I used to watch Max spinning his diabolo on the string, and I always was drawn to it. So, one day, when I went over to his house, I tried it. Max taught me some tricks, and I slowly got better. I felt good doing it. It is soothing and very rhythmic. We went to Boyle Park and practiced on the green grass in the sunshine. Max started one diabolo on the string, and then I passed the other diabolo to him. That day, I learned my first trick: a trapeze. Six months later, I stood in front of the audience for my eighth-grade project, feeling very nervous. However, as soon as I started doing my routine, all my nervousness fell away, and I was in my element. The diabolo is like life. You have to keep it spinning, or it will fall off. If you spin it too fast, it gets tangled in the string. In the same way, you have to keep working to keep your life balanced in an artful and graceful way.

Scientifically based information about the importance of play for healthy development is abundant, yet our schools continue to replace creative play with academic worksheets in our kindergartens as well as shortening or eliminating recesses and all subjects where play is a significant aspect (physical education, music, drama, art, etc.). Such policies stunt the development of children's intelligence, resilience, and adaptability and limit their capacities as well as the potential futures that they might have co-created. Again, there are no tests to assess the extent of the damage to children or its long-term effects on the resilience and creativity of our communities.

PLAYTIME

1. **Protect kindergarten children from premature academics by developing an active, play-based program.** Learning to cooperate and play with other children is an important life skill. This activity is particularly important for young children who have spent playtime at home watching screens. Schedule abundant time for free play in addition to teacher-led play activities.

2. **Increase recess up and down the grades.** An hour of free time each day is optimal for the elementary grades. Allow fifteen minutes between classes for older students — time to go to the bathroom, get a drink, stretch, connect with friends, and reset. This will also help teachers, who have similar needs and may need to connect with individual students before or after classes.

3. **Consider shortening the day to four hours for first and second graders.** Young children are tired by lunchtime. Many of them still need naps. Let them go home or enter a program that allows them to rest, eat, and play. These scheduling options are the rule in Finnish schools, which have the highest overall student performance based on international norms in the world.

4. **Incorporate movement, games, and physical activities into lessons throughout the day.**

5. **Incorporate playful solutions to solve problems.** My rambunctious first graders had difficulty with transitions. I told them a story about how Mother Deer taught her fawns to freeze and be still if she sensed a danger. From then on, I could say "Danger!" and get instant compliance — everyone would freeze. Then I would tell them to decide what kind of animal they were and to see if they could crawl, hop, run, slither, or fly to their seats without making any noise. Magical. By the time they reached their seats, they were focused and ready for a new activity.

6. **Respect free play in which children decide what they are going to do, set goals, and navigate challenges.** The American Academy of Pediatrics states that unstructured free play is so important for optimal child development that it has been recognized by the UN High Commission for Human Rights as a right of every child.

7. **Observe children at play to glean information about each child, their strengths and their challenges and how best to address them.**

For Parents: Play with your children. Turn off all screens. Participate in games, playful interactions, and make believe. Let your children set the rules and pretend to be the parents for a change. Respect their playtime and don't interrupt unless necessary. Watch, listen, and learn.

. . . . .

Children use play to overcome fear and to work through challenges. Research and observation tell us that strong attached relationships, plenty of physical activity, and a developmentally appropriate curriculum filled with play-based, hands-on activities can work miracles when it comes to healing trauma and removing impediments to learning. Something has gone seriously wrong when schools do not offer these natural solutions and instead support medicating children to get higher API scores or manage their restlessness at their desks. It is past time for a change.

We must stop looking at play as something children do in their free time and begin to understand that play has more to do with a state of mind than it does with specific activities. Dr. Brown defines play as "an absorbing, apparently purposeless activity that provides enjoyment and a suspension of self-consciousness and sense of time." The ultimate outgrowth of children's social play finds expression as the human brain playfully creates art and culture, essential to community survival. Music, dance, painting, and theater are intrinsic to the festivals and celebrations that bring people together "to sing with one voice."[54] I think at once of the Festival of Dionysus in ancient Athens, where the entire community gathered every year to participate with the actors, dancers, and musicians to enact plays by Sophocles, Aeschylus, Aristophanes (and numerous playwrights whose work has been lost), introducing the world to tragedy and comedy, engendering laughter, pity, and terror that echo down through the ages.

Chapter Seven

The Arts Are Not Extra

MORNING AT THE CABIN IN MENDOCINO
(with instructions NOT to wake Mom up)

The sky's like Creation
In a way
Because in the morning, like Creation,
The sky is all gray.
With a "Let there be light"
There's a streak of it
You can't see the sun,
But you know it's lit.
Remember "Let there be color"?
Well, look in the morning.
You should see the clouds ARE red
If you're not snoring.
Then there was Blue
Well, the sky itself turns color.
At this point it is SO amazing
You'd go and get your mother.
You're looking for yellow,
But the sun starts to rise,
And yellow light starts
Shimmering in the skies.

So, then there were plants,
But look all around,
There's tall trees in the sky
And grass on the ground.
Then God made Animals.
You heard a bird coo.
There's also a deer,
Looking straight at you
Then God made Humans.
You look at your mom.
You look at her from head to toe
You look at her palm to palm.
That's why the sky Is like Creation.
This shall go on
For Duration.

—**Nate,** age nine

Teachers are witnesses to wonders, surprises, and blessings as capacities unfold. Nate gave me this poem at the beginning of fourth grade. It tells me that the creation story Nate heard and painted with watercolors at the beginning of third grade sank in deep and is now lighting up his world. Again, this was all the assessment I needed. This capacity for making connections that Nate demonstrated so wonderfully wakes up in children when they are around nine years old with a noticeable change in consciousness. Children at nine are thinking about things in a new way. Teachers notice and respond by asking new kinds of questions and providing the children with opportunities to experience and then reflect on those experiences. This is the dance of the classroom, of learning and teaching, an art that cannot be scripted and measured any more than a work of art can be created by painting by numbers.

When I Googled the question "Are the arts essential to education?" there were hundreds of entries, many of them from reputable sources (the *New York Times*, the *Smithsonian*) that reported that the arts are indeed essential to learning and are integral to developing capacities such as creativity, self-confidence, problem solving, perseverance, focus, collaboration, memory, and responsibility. We now have scientific proof that playing music, writing poetry and stories, acting, painting, drawing, and dancing affect the way our brains develop and facilitate greater learning in all subjects. In spite of all the evidence, however, the arts continue to be seen as non-essential "extras" in our schools. They are dropped during budget crises or cut back to make more time in the schedule for academic subjects.

Granted, there is no objective way to assess artistic capacities on a multiple-choice test. Because funding and teacher evaluation are linked to test scores, the test makers, who may know very little about children or how they learn, are determining a curriculum heavily focused on math, science, and information analysis but bereft of the arts.

However, when we ask what sort of education today's children will need to meet the enormous challenges posed by climate and system change, we find ourselves listing capacities such as creativity, self-confidence, ability to solve problems, perseverance, focus, collaborative skills, empathy, and willingness to sacrifice for the common good. Unless we understand how these capacities are fostered and strengthened by the arts and make them an essential aspect of the way we educate children, we run the risk of losing our souls as well as our life-supporting biosphere.

The arts are integral to what it means to be human. Their value goes far beyond supporting success in more academic subjects. Human beings painted and drew pictures long before they invented writing; indeed, the first writing grew out of such pictures. They made music and danced to that beat from time immemorial as a means of both expression and intention. They enacted the hunt, the harvest, and marriage as rituals that ensured continuity and survival. All small children across the world reenact these gestures through play, through the pictures they draw, the songs they sing, and the stories they enact. This is how we learn and practice how to be human—through imitation in its various forms. This is how we celebrate our humanness together. This is how we find our bearings on our human journey. The kind of human being that we become has everything to do with the quality of these artistic experiences and the quality of the truths that the artists in our midst are able to share with the rest of us.

Chris Hedges writes in his *Truthdig* essay "How to Think":

> *There are, as Shakespeare wrote, "things invisible to mortal sight." But these things are not vocational or factual or empirical. They are not found in national myths of glory and power. They are not attained by force. They do not come through cognition or logical reasoning. They are intangible. They are the realities of beauty, grief, love, the search for meaning, the struggle to face our own mortality, and the ability to face truth. And cultures that disregard these forces of imagination commit suicide. A society that marginalizes the arts and suppresses artists runs the risk of becoming lost and self-destructive.*[55]

It is not surprising that a culture that promotes individualism, sees achievement as winning after intense competition, and measures success by the amount of money that one makes does not value the arts, which are at their core communal celebrations. The struggle for meaning that animates artists is, first and foremost, a desire to communicate: to share a vision, a perspective, an experience with others.

Whether we are on the receiving end of creation as the audience, creating something ourselves — a poem, a painting, a song — or joining with others to co-create, we are participating in a shared experience. These shared experiences form the contents of our consciousness as well as our values. They are essential to education, both in the practice of the various arts and in the reciprocal experience of learning to be a discerning and engaged audience.

Learning how to cooperate and be an effective member of a community while expressing one's creative individuality is a fruitful dynamic that should be the basis of our educational system.

Waldorf schools offer arts-based education. This means that arts of all kinds — creative play, music, visual arts, drama, dance, poetry, creative writing, carving and modeling, cooking, sewing, knitting, and crocheting — are integrated into the daily lessons. I asked some former students, now young adults who have recently graduated from college, what their early experience with the arts meant to them. They acknowledged that they took it for granted and thought this was how school was supposed to be.

Hannah went to a public school for the first few years of high school:

> *It was not until I transferred to the San Francisco Waldorf High School that I realized what I had lost. The opportunity to weave arts through my day suddenly lit up my education once again. Creativity on every level, expression in so many forms, this is what my childhood was full of, and I never realized it.*

Lily wrote:

> *There is something truly unique about creating something or participating in something creative that does not compare to anything else. Indeed, whether or not one has that "natural creativity," there is a confidence that is derived by engaging in artistic expression. Making and creating is felt in a different part of your body and soul. Hearing that harmony come together in a song, or feeling the plaster take form under your touch, brings you to an entirely different dimension.*

Kaleb wrote that his experience with the arts helped him appreciate the effort needed to make objects and what it means to have tables, benches, and chairs. *I know the effort that is required to handcraft those things, and because of that, I have an appreciation for them.* He also noted that he believed his practice in the arts had made him a smarter, more adaptive young adult:

> *My past experience with such a wide array of different arts allows me to be good at deducing how to do new things, even with no prior knowledge. This means I can adapt to many situations quickly and can acquire and learn new skills very easily.*

Max made the connection between his creative education and his later cognitive skills:

> *The creativity I experienced as a child has helped me keep a balanced life. Throughout university, I made time to play music, to attend theater, and to question. Questioning is born out of being encouraged to think for myself and to develop my own perspectives. While more academic than knitting a pair of socks, questioning the status quo is imperative to solving problems.... Being given the opportunity, the freedom, to use the creative side of my brain and to engage with the arts as a child has enabled me to succeed in all areas of my life (academics, work environments, relationships). For that, I am deeply thankful.*

Michael described his experience of first performing in public:

> *It was bright onstage, and I could hardly see the profile of what seemed to be the most giant audience ever. It was the first time I had been nervous about performing, even though we had practiced for an entire month on the one song we were about to play. I walked on stage with my guitar, followed by Dante with his bass and Justin and Kaleb on the drums. It seemed the most suspenseful moment of my life, the rustle of guitar chords and other equipment as we prepared to play and then silence, dead silence. I couldn't breathe. But as soon as we started to play in front of an audience for the first time, my shoulders dropped, Dante and I looked at each other, and it was complete ecstasy from then on. I will never forget the experience of that performance or the people I got to share that experience with.*

In his famous TED talk, which has had over 31 million views, Sir Ken Robinson tells us, "An aesthetic experience is one in which your senses are operating at their peak: when you're present in the current moment; when you're resonating with the excitement of this thing you are experiencing; when you are fully alive." An eloquent and humorous spokesman for the essential role of arts in education, he says things like "Creativity is as important as literacy" and "Our only hope for the future is to adopt a new concept of human ecology that is based on the richness of human capacity." He compares our contemporary fixation on science, math, and textual analysis with strip mining. Everyone in the TED audience laughs and claps.[56]

My involvement in university theater opened a new door to the world, offering not only the opportunity to co-create with others but also a way to practice becoming my "self." I loved taking acting, directing, and playwriting classes and doing something challenging every day instead of just sitting and listening to professors talk. My father worried about what I might do with a degree in theater, but he didn't need to fret. It was the best possible preparation for my eventual career in education.

I had to stretch to be able to teach drawing and painting, and I learned to play the recorder along with my students, but what could be better than having eight years to shape my lively, playful class into a troupe of skilled actors and actresses? They came to me with their imaginations fired up by kindergarten play and stories, more than ready to act those stories out.

In first grade, I adapted a Chinese fairy tale, "SuLang and the Dragon Princess." Most of the children couldn't read yet, but they had the play memorized by the time I had read it through to them several times. I remember Theron, one of my quieter boys, announcing to me that he was the Dragon King. We even had an Octopus Chorus. (The tale takes place under the sea.) We sat in a circle, with the audience sitting around us, and the children came to the center to act their parts. The class spoke in chorus to narrate the story, and each character with lines had a partner who stood up from the circle and spoke in unison with them. This gave support to the first graders who felt shy in the presence of parents and other students. I do remember that SuLang was so overcome at one point that he played his recorder with his shirt pulled over his head. But true love prevailed after many challenges, and this play about the magic of music was a resounding success!

In second grade, in the woodland area adjacent to our playground, we performed a play that told of the coming of St. Patrick to Ireland. We had dancing forest nymphs, druids, painted warriors, and wonderful Celtic songs. The children had grown tremendously in confidence and could now take speaking parts on their own. I had cast Joey as St. Patrick, and his mother told me of a conversation with him. She had asked him if I had given him the main part because I knew he could remember all of the lines, and he told her, "No! Mrs. Cummings gave me the part because Patrick is close to God and she knows that I am close to God, too."

For the third grade, I wrote a play for the children called *Joseph in Two Lands,* telling the story of Joseph and his brothers. Jealousy, betrayal, suffering, redemption, and finally, forgiveness seemed potent themes for nine-year-old third graders to take on. By now, the children could follow conventional staging and handle their backstage costume changes and props by themselves. I could sometimes hear their intense whispers as they gave each other *sotto voce* reminders.

Charissa Drengsen, a parent, wrote our fourth-grade play. I had reassured her when the Catholics prevailed in second grade that the pagans would have their day. She made sure that the girls had major roles as Valkyries and strong Norse women.

In fifth grade, we enacted the adventures of Perseus, with roles for gods, heroes, and various interesting creatures like Medusa. By now, the children were commended by everyone for their clarity of speech and their timing. We could no longer hear the backstage whispers.

In sixth grade, the class was ready for a major challenge. Nate's mother, Leslie Currier, and I adapted *Arabian Nights,* a play she had written for the Marin Shakespeare Festival. Charissa Drengsen and a friend, who happened to be a professional set builder, turned our outdoor amphitheater into a domed backdrop with multiple levels and entrances. Gary Malkin, Genny's gifted musician father, enlisted several Middle Eastern musicians to play with him during and between the scenes. The children took multiple roles as they enacted the stories told by Scheherazade to her vengeful husband. They managed backstage on their own, their voices loud and clear, and their comic timing honed to the audience's frequent laughter. I could just sit in the audience and be a very inwardly active spectator. The following is an excerpt from an article that I wrote for the school newsletter:

> *Last summer, I had compelling reasons to choose* One Thousand and One Arabian Nights *as the subject of our sixth-grade play. Scheherazade transforms the darkness that has gripped her world through her gift of storytelling and her ability to love in the face of fear and danger. I wanted the children to live into and embody this message of courage and hope and to celebrate the transformative power of stories and theater. I also wanted to offer the children a positive experience of Arab culture as part of our study of the Middle Ages. Theater is magical. Time and space melt away when we put on turbans or swirling veils and enact marvelous tales of adventure, love, and the foibles of ordinary people. We meet Abu Kassim, struggling unsuccessfully to get rid of his stinking sandals, Aladdin, turning from a disobedient scamp into a young man worthy of a princess, and Scheherazade herself as she transforms a terrible fate into a brilliant destiny by writing a new story instead of becoming a victim of Shahryar's obsession. These vibrant characters touch us, make us laugh and weep with their humanity, allow us to see ourselves in new ways, and, in turn, demolish the stereotypes that promote seeing whole groups of people as "the enemy." As the Storyteller tells his young captors at the end of the play, "May this story enter through a crack in our hearts, transforming our world and us, like Scheherazade's love entered into and transformed her husband's soul, restoring Sasan as the Kingdom of Forgiveness and Shahryar as the King of All Joy."*

During our final two years together, we rented a theater and did full-scale productions of Shakespeare's *Midsummer Night's Dream* and Thornton Wilder's *The Skin of Our Teeth*. By this time, I had a troupe of young actors that any ensemble would be proud of. Several of them later became actors, directors, and playwrights, but for all of them, this was a learning ground, providing experiences that charted multidimensional growth. Here are Hannah's and Lily's memories of that process:

In my first memory of our many plays, I am a Viking. I think I'm the princess. I'm definitely in charge and very important. So important I died. Or rather, went into a coma the entire play... until the very end. Now, here's the kicker: Rory kissed my hand (he really kissed his own thumb, tricks of the elementary school trade), and I woke up. However, I had to endure the misery of cooties. A boy's mouth that close to my hand? Disgusting.

Flash forward to sixth grade, and Allison drops out. You told me you knew I could handle taking on her role in the play on top of my own. With only days to prepare, I decided you were wrong. Very wrong. I remember going home and crying and practicing my new lines on my back deck and feeling overwhelmed, to say the least. Looking back, it was one of those moments when you pushed me to do something I wasn't sure I could handle. The lines were learned, the play performed, and I learned that I perform well under pressure. I still cry when I'm overwhelmed, sad, happy, and laughing, but I always perform in a time crunch.

Seventh grade: I can't remember a single word of it, but I remember singing the fairy lullaby. Singing. About fairies. This is not good for a girl going through puberty. The best part of the performance locked in my memories is not the performance at all but the playhouse itself. The feeling of independence being backstage. The nooks and graffiti-covered walls. It all felt so grown up, but now I see it was all fairies running around in the dark, and that picture is even better than the reality of the playhouse filled with disruptive rabies bats.

The Skin of Our Teeth *was, of course, my shining moment. I don't know why I suddenly wanted to forget my stage fright and take the lead. To this day, it's the biggest speaking role I've ever had onstage. I guess what this all boils down to are experiences that pushed us out of our comfort zones. Experiences that forced us to work as a team but also let a single member shine, and in doing so, we shone together. All of these roles, from half-dead Viking princess to dramatic maid, were just preparing us for our much bigger roles. My next one is on Wall Street.*

—Hannah

I was recently reminiscing about performing A Midsummer Night's Dream. I remember you cast me as Puck, and I felt so thrilled to have such a prominent role. It was a great challenge but such a rewarding experience, realizing I could memorize the many lines and play the role convincingly. You always would cast the parts with such thought and intention, giving everyone the opportunity to play one of the primary roles in at least one of the plays over the years. In that same production, I remember Liam and Kaya were cast together as one of the pairs of lovers, which was truly the opposite of their actual relationship. I do believe it helped them work through their tense friendship in some ways, or at least find some inner strength to put aside their animosity for a while. And that wasn't an isolated situation. There were many occasions where the roles you'd so thoughtfully selected required us to work on how we interacted as individuals with one another. It allowed people to grow in many ways personally as well, providing us all with the opportunity to portray different aspects of our inner selves that may not have come to light without your directing guidance.

—Lily

Lily and Hannah point to our theater experiences as a primary platform for self-discovery and personal growth as well as an opportunity to strengthen community—our ability to collaborate and create together in spite of differences. I witnessed this dual process of awakening individual creativity through intense and purposeful collaboration repeatedly throughout my years as a teacher.

Each teacher has special talents and interests that can inspire students, but it is equally important for teachers to model a willingness to take risks and appear less than proficient. I began by copying drawings done by other teachers who were more skilled than I but soon attempted my own. When I did an especially good drawing, the children noticed and celebrated my progress. My voice has a very limited singing range, but I could play the piano and learned to play the recorder. We sang in parts, played an instrument, or recited poetry every morning for eight years! By seventh grade, some of my students, who were more skilled than I am, illustrated the lessons on the chalkboard for the class.

Although there are protocols for essays and term papers, creative writing is primarily a personal process that develops with practice. Beyond the spelling, grammar, and mechanics, there is a voice that is discovering what it has to say to others. Ideally, this voice will be as distinctive as its unique source. In the writings above, Lily's and Hannah's voices are very different and instantly recognizable to anyone who knows them. A system that rewards the regurgitation of information and the ideas of others, that grades and corrects "papers" and has little interest in what students have to say, will not help students discover what they want to communicate. The tragic result is that many people seem to feel they have nothing to contribute. They feel essentially invisible and unknown, even to themselves.

I met Jim in one of my Y-, bottom-track sophomore English classes. I remember his name when all other names from that time have faded because I can still see it scrawled across the page in increasingly large letters from the left side all the way to the right. Jim was an attractive boy who wore his white t-shirt sleeves rolled up to show off his emerging biceps. I don't remember that he handed in many assignments, but I do remember engaging the class in writing haiku poetry, which I collected, printed, collated, and distributed as little poetry books. Years later, at an event at Contra Costa Junior College, I was hailed across the room by a taller, bearded version of Jim. He came to me, gave me a hug, and told me that he had dropped out of high school and enlisted in the Army. He had been in Viet Nam, come home, and finished his G.E.D. Now he was graduating from the J.C. and going on to one of the state colleges. Jim grinned and said, "You'll never guess what I am planning to do. I want to be an English teacher! And you know, it all started in your class. Do you remember having us write those poems? When I saw my poem, all printed up with my name under it, it really hit me. I can write and have other people read what I have to say! It had never occurred to me before, and I never forgot it. I began to write when I was in Nam. Thank you."

Clayton joined our class in sixth grade — an unusually tall, gangly boy with a great sense of humor and a tendency to avoid doing schoolwork. Clayton underperformed academically, although he was a wonderful actor and active participant in all of our adventures. Getting at whatever was impeding him was challenging. He would break out with painful eczema if he felt pressured. I told Clayton and his parents that I had no doubt about his basic capacities and that Clayton would have to find motivation to study from inside himself. Time passed. In seventh grade, I asked the class to write a Shakespearean sonnet — a challenging assignment for any age.

Clayton handed in the following sonnet:

> *Oh, when the birds on gray wings fly too far*
> *And vision is lost in the thick myst of dark time,*
> *The feet sink fast as if in thick black tar*
> *And food in mouth tastes sour and foul as lime.*
> *The crystal life blood of our very being*
> *Now soiled with ashes lies spewed upon the ground.*
> *We are blind to what we should be seeing.*
> *The hardened earth in anger we do pound.*
> *The end here comes as fast as your doomed death.*
> *Two times three hundred signs we failed to read*
> *And now we die, we die with pain and grief.*

We did not change our ways and now you heed:
All of our striving, strengthening for a better life
Will kill us and the world with our own knife.

I was stunned when I read this poem and told Clayton that he had totally "blown his cover." No wonder he resisted. For a boy this young to see so deeply and to express such despair was remarkable. Reading it over, I am still amazed by his prescience. When I read the poem aloud, the class was able to look at Clayton with a much deeper understanding. We could glimpse what was incubating behind his good-humored goofiness, his sometimes-sudden need for quiet and protection. This was also a pivotal moment for Clayton. He began to accomplish more, to step more confidently into his life.

Reading over Clayton's sonnet, I can also see the impact of a great mentor: Shakespeare, whose poetry was performed every morning by my students. I had given each student a sonnet or a speech from a Shakespearean play as a birthday verse to memorize and recite once a week at the beginning of class. Yes, twenty-seven Shakespearean verses were learned effortlessly by heart by everyone before the year was over! Copying someone is usually considered pejorative, but a much deeper process of *mimesis* seems to be at work here. Looking up this word — *mimesis* — in the dictionary reminds me of Esme's discovery: that even after you have read all the definitions of a word of power, you still don't know everything it means. We learn by imitating, not merely copying but taking something in deeply, allowing it to inform us, to shape our experience, to affect the way we see and respond to the world. Great artists like Shakespeare have this power to shape us, to deeply educate and inspire us, and to help us realize our human powers of expression.

Actively practicing various modes of artistic expression develops a long list of capacities that underlie individuality and personal success. Reciprocally, learning to be a receptive audience for the artistic expression of others builds capacities like empathy and moral sensibility that underlie healthy community. Together, these roles, creative and receptive, shape our humanity and determine the health of our souls, our society, and our planet.

I recently had an experience that brought me in touch with the living reality behind these somewhat abstract words. I was invited to be in the audience for a concert that celebrated a musical reunion of three women who had not sung together publicly for more than a decade. Tenaya, Sophia, and Alyx were young high school students when I first heard them singing *a Capella* in close harmony in the chemistry laboratory during lunch hours. They wrote their own songs, and their blended voices were distinctive. Copper Wimmin sang together for a number of years, produced three CDs that can be accessed on YouTube, and won music awards, and then its members parted to pursue separate interests. Delighted to see and hear them together once again, I was deeply moved to witness how each one has grown in depth and range without losing their connection. The collective courage that allowed them to experiment and innovate musically as teenagers is still in evidence, as is their shared social conscience. They wrapped me up in their songs and gave me a precious gift: the opportunity to witness that their creative explorations as children are serving them well as mature, creative women, whether they continue to perform together or not.[57]

Being a member of the audience can be a life-changing experience. I remember going with my father to see *The Last of the Mohicans*. I must have been nine or ten, on the brink of a new level of consciousness that awoke through the strong imagery and disturbing events of that film. I remember feeling deeply outraged by the massacre and upset that people could do such things to one another. From then on, my education from serious literature was at sharp odds with the mythology of Saturday matinee cowboys and Indians and the sanitized social studies lessons I received in school.

I took two of my grandchildren (at ages eleven and fourteen) to see *Selma,* a film reflecting events leading up to the march from Selma to Montgomery during the 1965 voting rights movement. We were transported to Selma by director Ava Duvernay to agonize with Martin Luther King over the decisions he had to make. We listened to arguments among the leaders of King's Southern Leadership Conference and the young activists from the Student Nonviolent

Coordinating Committee. The audience held its breath as we stood with the marchers on the bridge, cringed and gasped as the blows began to fall, and then moved forward with them in solidarity as collective courage trumped personal fear. Afterward, we were left to reflect individually on the cruelty that human beings are capable of and the courage and commitment required to make real change. We had experienced the force of an idea whose time and place had arrived. We watched this courage and commitment ignite a group of individuals into a community of action.

I wished that there had been a forum for audience members to talk about what they had witnessed and experienced, something I did on the way home with my grandchildren. I regretted that this film wasn't available when my class studied the civil rights movement.

I was heartened to hear that a group of black businessmen passed the hat and made it possible for every middle-school-aged child in New York City to see *Selma* for free. They must have felt that it was essential for their education. What if we showed the film to every middle and high school child in America and used it to begin a conversation critical to the survival of our democracy? How many children might begin to question and think for themselves? No wonder some of those in power are interested in co-opting and controlling the content of the curriculum from kindergarten through college. No wonder they fear and would eliminate the power of the arts.

USE THE ARTS TO BRING LEARNING ALIVE

1. **Be brave and participate fully in all artistic activities.** Teachers are models for children and must be willing to strive as novices in all artistic endeavors as well as share their talents.

2. **Draw or paint illustrations for the stories that you tell.** When students give form to what they have imagined, memory and imagination are strengthened. Children can draw with crayons or colored pencils or paint their own illustrations rather than copying the teacher's, although copying should also be an option for children who lack confidence.

3. **Encourage students to explore various media**—wood carving, clay, plaster, metalwork, fiber—either through regular art periods or as projects for science or history. You can also use such materials to illustrate ideas. For example, when I wanted high school students to begin to grasp the qualitative differences between the materially based Later Roman Empire and the more inwardly inspired Early Middle Ages, I gave each student a fist-sized block of clay. I told them to shape it into a square while I described how the Roman public buildings in each town were turned into churches, and we discussed the possible social and emotional change this transition entailed. At the end of our discussion, I asked them to make a depression on one side of the square, turning the Roman speaker's dais into a baptismal font, a symbol for the birth of a new consciousness, a going inward. I got this idea from another teacher. The possibilities are endless, particularly when a group of inspired teachers begins to share.

4. **Strengthen memory by reciting poetry or important speeches alone or with a group.** That we describe this process as "learning by heart" is telling. What we learn by heart, we tend to remember all our lives. In her late eighties, my grandmother Della could still recite all of Longfellow's *Evangeline,* a long poem she had learned by heart in her one-room school as a child.

5. **Sing in harmony or play a simple instrument at the beginning of each school day.** The music can reflect the curriculum, the seasons, or the holidays. This is time well spent, bringing the children firmly into the school day and their work together. As they become more mature, choosing an instrument and playing together in a school orchestra or band is an experience that all children should have. I know of no better way to practice forming a harmonious community of gifted individuals.

6. **Weave creative assignments into homework or take-home tests on course content.** Allow students to choose whether to write an essay, poem, or story, give a speech, or compose a song.

Test day(s) can then be filled with everyone's creative insights and expressions.

7. **Check out Bates Middle School in Maryland.** Bates was struggling in 2007. Teachers were demoralized, and student achievement was down. Starting in 2008, faculty, staff, and students began to transform their school by integrating the arts through all subjects. You can read about the results of this transformation in improved academic performance as well as student and faculty enthusiasm for learning.[58]

> **For Parents: Practice art.** Paint, draw, play an instrument, sing, act, sculpt, arrange flowers, express whatever gives you pleasure. You are a model for your child. If you do not have a particular artistic skill, choose one and begin.

. . . . .

Emeritus Education Professor Bill Ayers reimagines school in his book *Demand the Impossible: A Radical Manifesto:*

> *Education, then, is transformed from rote boredom and endlessly alienating routines into something that is eye-popping and mind-blowing — always opening doors and opening minds and opening hearts as students forge their own pathways into a wider world.*[59]

Practicing the arts opens our minds and hearts to our deepest questions, the questions that motivate us to do everything in our power to find answers and deepen our understanding.

Chapter Eight

We Learn by Asking Questions

THE REAL WORK
It may be that when we no longer know what to do
we have come to our real work
and when we no longer know which way to go
we have begun our real journey.
The mind that is not baffled is not employed.
The impeded stream is the one that sings.
           —Wendell Berry, *Collected Poems*

I began writing this book by asking myself a question: what do I know from my own experience about how children learn? This inquiry led me on a path of discovery. I could see that my early questions about how our education system might better serve students shaped the choices I made, including my most recent decision to sit hours a day at my computer, striving to share what I have learned instead of "enjoying my retirement."

My questions, however, are like food. They power both my sense of myself and my connection and responsibility to others; they get me up in the morning and charge my day. What can I do to help this child? How can I make a difference in my community? What is the right action to take on this issue? How can I find an image or a story that will help my readers feel as well as know what I am describing?

I can't imagine not being beset by questions, searches for information, and periods of reflection.

Young human beings are naturally inquisitive. One of their signal achievements in early childhood is asking questions. From age three on, there is a creative tension between "learning to do what you are told"—being obedient—and questioning.

Children from several generations fondly remember the elephant in Rudyard Kipling's "Elephant's Child," who was spanked frequently by his elders for his *"satiable curtiosity."* How pleased we were to hear that this adventurous, inquisitive pachyderm, as a result of his disobedience, learned how to turn the tables on his elders by using his new trunk to spank them back. Healthy preschool children may ask hundreds of questions a day, a process that accompanies an explosion of new brain synapses and connections, estimated at a quadrillion—three times more than in the adult brain.

One of my favorite memories of this phase in my family occurred on Angel Island in San Francisco Bay. Our twin boys were three at the time, and we had docked our sailboat to wait out a sudden change in the weather. We heard foghorns begin to bellow as we hiked around the island in a stiff breeze. Tim was startled and asked what was making that noise. He was silent for a few minutes after I told him it was a foghorn. Then he asked, "What does the foghorn do?" His father told him to think about it. A few minutes later, Tim answered, "It scares away the fog." We suppressed our laughter and did not correct him. A few minutes later, another question: "How does the fog have ears?" Making sense of the world is a challenging process. This story is amusing and memorable because it illustrates a developing human capacity—the growing ability to make sense of the world through following a set of questions. Every young child is on this urgent quest.

Kindergarten and first-grade children are still full of questions that are most likely to spill out in casual conversation. Questions that engaged our whole class often started as they ate their snacks or lunches, particularly on stormy days when they weren't focused on getting out to the playground as quickly as possible. I remember one earnest debate about whether it was best to be cremated or buried when you died, as well as a priceless first-grade conversation described in one of my weekly parent letters:

> Kelly had brought in a beautiful picture book of the constellations the day before, and I read and showed it to the class. They were very interested to know about their particular constellations. These became the topic of the next afternoon's chat. After some discussion, someone asked if constellations ever change, and Rory replied that they do but very slowly. Then he gave an example by holding up his arm, saying that Orion's arm might move just a little bit in 1,000 years. Someone wondered about stars and whether or not they ever die. A hubbub of conversation ensued, which was capped by Michael saying, "Yes, they do. They die of starvation!" There was total silence for a moment, and then Heather's great laugh as she said, "Don't you get it? Star-vation?"

What an incredible leap children make in just a few years, from framing their first tentative questions to being able to invent and appreciate riddles and jokes. I made it a point through the years to find out what my students knew before starting to teach a new subject.

Their answers and questions often took my lessons in new directions while providing important information about individual children. Although, for the most part, my students did not determine our course of study, I wanted them to feel that we were on a joint inquiry of shared information and knowledge, even in the lower grades.

The following parent letters recount how my second graders and I first learned about multiplication:

Dear Parents,

I want to tell you more about the math unit on multiplication that we are beginning. I have been trying to find a balance between giving the children a variety of experiences that build clear concepts and providing them with sufficient practice in computation. I was very pleased this morning to find them enthusiastic about starting our math block. "Good," someone said. "I like playing those games and working together."

We began by asking, "What is multiplication?" After an initial discussion, I asked everyone to write an explanation. The results ranged from detailed (and correctly solved) word problems to a poignant "I would tell you the answer, but my brain just won't work this morning." A delightful drawing of a confused brain accompanied this entry. One responder launched into the discussion by saying that multiplication was times. "For example, you could have the numbers three and two. Say that three is three cows and two is two chickens. Then you would have five animals. I think that is multiplication."

I hope that by the end of our block, we will have demystified multiplication. We will be investigating real-life situations, looking at geometric models and numerical patterns. The children will be exploring with manipulatives, writing multiplication story problems, and playing games. We ended this morning by listing things that come in 2s—eyes, hands, chopsticks, wheels, slices of bread for a sandwich, hoops on a basketball court, etc. Tomorrow, we will think of things that come in 3s, 4s, 5s, and so on up to 12. We will use the items on our lists to pose problems: How many wheels are there on five tricycles? How many feet are in our class?

We can also generate multiples. If one spider has 8 legs, then 6 spiders have 48 legs, etc.

So, instead of teaching the facts and procedures of multiplication as abstractions and logarithms, I am designing experiences that will engage the children actively. If any of you would like to visit before the year's end, this will be an interesting time to come....

(Two weeks pass.)

In spite of our coughs, sniffles and sore throats, the second graders and I have been having an excellent time with multiplication. This week, they wrote story problems with some very improbable stories involving creatures from Planet BX with numerous eyes. There was also an amusing tale about a lady with fat feet who either needed to divide her feet or find fat shoes.

On Wednesday, these story problems were read aloud while two students stood at the board ready 1) to write the problem in numbers and 2) to solve it. Everyone had their turns at the board and reading. By the end, they had solved 24 multiplication problems! Even better, they had demonstrated that they know what multiplication is for.

As a student from elementary school through university, I became accustomed to answering teacher-generated questions, usually requiring some form of regurgitation. This could be challenging, interesting, or a terribly boring ordeal, depending on the teacher, but I don't remember there being much space for my questions or even interest in knowing what they were. If I didn't understand something, I tended to be quiet about it and hope that the light would eventually dawn.

Unfortunately, I also learned to keep many of my thoughts and questions to myself rather than responding openly to assignments.

I had been profoundly upset by being accused of plagiarism in fifth grade. I had read and wept many tears over W. H. Hudson's *Green Mansions* and, inspired by Hudson's rather florid style, written a long book report that signaled a moment of painful discovery for my nine-year-old heart and mind. My fifth-grade teacher, Mr. Maxwell, called me aside and informed me that I couldn't have read the book or written the report. He didn't believe my protestations, and it took a visit from my mother to set him straight. I realized through this experience that he didn't see me at all, and my memory of him stops at that point.

I was accused again of plagiarism during my sophomore year at UC Berkeley. The professor told me that I had written an outstanding paper, so outstanding, in fact, that he felt that I must have plagiarized at least some of it. I challenged him to find the original and told him that if he couldn't, he had no business questioning my work. I won but felt deeply disrespected, both as a woman (I had only one female professor in all my years at UC Berkeley!) and as a student. That I remember both incidents so vividly underscores how damaging it is to be falsely accused instead of validated and seen. How different these interactions would have been if these teachers had asked me questions to find out if their suspicions had merit.

In contrast, I was electrified by Dr. Cavell's philosophy of religion class, which I mentioned in Chapter Two. His presentations respected my latent and emergent abilities, and his assignments offered me an opportunity to follow his example by framing and answering questions of my own. At last! "What do we mean when we say that a belief is deep?" he asked. I had never thought about language in this way, and I could literally feel my brain growing as I attempted to imitate and initiate the questioning process he was demonstrating. I wrote two papers. The first explored the paradox inherent in forgiveness (taking away that which exists), and the second explored what it means to be "born again," comparing religious conversion to how actors bring characters to life by using Camus's assertion that *there is no frontier between being and appearing*. These are the only undergraduate essays that I remember writing. Dr. Cavell enjoyed them. Writing these papers changed me and inspired my later intentions as a teacher to be a model for asking questions rather than a fountain of predetermined answers.

Learning how to do that was often a struggle, given the depth of my own educational conditioning. It is much easier to follow sets of information with questions at the end of the chapter. It is less challenging to present information and then assess students on how accurately they can feed it back. Testing, grading, and assessing whether or not students have learned essential information is a challenging process that, in the end, may say more about the teacher's performance than it does about the students.

Assessment is helpful for teachers to know what must be retaught or rediscussed, but even "A+'s" on regurgitated information do not indicate whether the students have taken ideas in, absorbed them, and connected them to other concerns or questions. I tried various approaches to deal with this problem. I wrote this Sunday-night letter to sixth-grade parents after the class had studied the Middle Ages:

Dear Parents,

Instead of a written test on the Middle Ages, I circled the children and told them we were going to have a formal discussion. They prepared for this by reflecting on their questions or observations about the time period between 400 and 1400 AD. First, we went around the circle, hearing from each student, and then took up the questions that seemed to have the most energy for the most children. How could something like the Children's Crusade happen? (The Children's Crusade was a disastrous undertaking in which thousands of young children died or were sold into slavery in Africa.) The other question we took up was a bit harder for them to formulate but had to do with the tendency of religion (a good thing) to lead to war (a bad thing) and what to do about it. I said very little and primarily conducted traffic.

A courteous and productive hour-long discussion ensued in which the children were able to come to some understanding of how such an event as the Children's Crusade could happen. The children suggested early marriage; short life spans, which also meant that children did not have protected childhoods; belief in visions and trust that God, who had called the children, would protect them; belief that sacrificing one's life for a noble cause was a good thing; and the practical suggestion that maybe the children came from big families that didn't mind having one less mouth to feed. This discussion also led to the question of how you could tell true visions from false ones. How could one know that a leader had truly had a vision? How could one tell if a holy person was real or a fake?

The second discussion was less focused but very lively. Most children thought that they would "know" if someone was truly holy if they could be physically near them. They would "feel" it. They struggled with the idea of "jihad." How could fighting and killing be part of a religion, and why do Christians mostly ignore Christ's injunction to "love their enemies"? Although it might be wonderful if everyone could have the same religion, they thought that this would never work. They observed that some religions could be combined: that Buddhism seems to mix well with other religions and not cause wars because Buddha didn't say that he was God's Messenger. They wondered about God's role in all this confusion and why he appeared differently to different people. And they touched on the evolution of consciousness. Is atheism a religion? Even within religions, people believe very differently. Why was the Church so worried about difference that they made the Inquisition? Why do we have to have religions at all?

Most felt that it is important to have one but not to fight about beliefs.

They were unanimous that they preferred "discussing" to test taking. Me, too. I wish all of you could have been flies on the wall. It's exciting to watch them begin to learn how to think together. The opportunity to think together on important questions with a group of peers that you know and trust is one of the very best aspects of education. When our Summerfield graduates came back from their first year of college, they often said that the discussions were disappointing, even in special programs like the Hutchins Humanities seminar program at Sonoma State University, because the other students didn't seem to know how to think for themselves or how to think together. They missed their Waldorf classmates.

The questions that my sixth graders quite naturally held about the Children's Crusade led to more complicated questions about the role religion has played and is currently playing in our human relationships. That there are no simple or "right" answers to such questions is painfully apparent as we watch countries in the Middle East devolve into violence and social chaos. Religious differences within sects of Islam and between Islamic and Christian societies have been activated and manipulated by all sides in a hegemonic struggle for power in the region. This conflict is one of the most perplexing and difficult challenges of our time. Yet, I do not remember my formal education through graduate school addressing this issue through thoughtful discussion, even in my history classes.

Americans are generally uninformed about the Arab world and the history of the Middle East and are, therefore, particularly vulnerable to propaganda and fearmongering. When I went to our local public library to look for information about Islam at the outbreak of the Persian Gulf War in 1990, I found only two books on the shelf. At the time, I was teaching high school classes in ancient and medieval history and realized how unprepared I was to help my students understand the religious, historical, and cultural precedents to current conflicts. Although a plethora of books on the Middle East is now available, I do not see much evidence that many Americans have done their homework and tried to understand the forces that are currently at play.

When I taught an extension course for teachers at Sonoma State University on how to teach history without textbooks, the teachers told me that they never mentioned or talked about religion with their students, that presenting information about Islam or Christianity was not allowed. This myopic understanding of the First Amendment's separation of church and state is unfortunately rampant, and teachers do not want to become targets for angry parents. So much for their students' questions and the possibility of an informed citizenry.

Our brains and our futures are shaped by the questions we ask (or don't ask). Being able to ask probing questions, listen thoughtfully to others, and follow a line of inquiry in a group discussion is an art that merits daily practice. If students are asked only to memorize answers to questions they have not generated themselves, they will get quite good at doing just that. The students that my Waldorf graduates encountered in college had developed different brains and skill sets. On the whole, they were not practiced at asking salient questions or thinking in concert with others. This limitation of many college graduates has been noted by frustrated employers, particularly in new technology industries.

Concern that our graduates would not be able to compete well in meeting the needs of employers is a driving logic behind the Common Core, which professes higher standards for critical thinking, problem solving, and analysis. The touted improvement of this test over its standardized predecessors was that the standards would spiral in complexity through the grades rather than being introduced as separate, disconnected subjects at chosen grade levels. The problem, of course, is that they are spiraled with little understanding of child development, of what children can accomplish at various ages, and they fail to address the basic issue—how capacities like critical thinking are actually fostered and developed. The only capacity that I am sure is fostered by the Common Core test is the ability to ferret out correct answers while surviving long days of testing.

Before inflicting yet another top-down process onto American students, we could have asked why so many middle and high school students have ceased to ask questions and express curiosity. Many public school students were frustrated in my classes because I wouldn't tell them precisely what they needed to know to get an "A." They were angry that I wouldn't give them a set of answers to go with a discrete set of questions and resented "wasting time" in open-ended class discussions.

The question is, did these children stop asking questions because they had lost interest beyond their immediate adolescent relationships and activities, or did they lose interest because the rote answers promoted by textbook and test-driven instruction do not encourage questioning or development of individual capacities and can even penalize students for attempting to do so?

Such students no longer expect to be seen or inspired by their teachers and may not be consciously aware of what they have lost or how their potential has been stunted or deformed. They may graduate into the workforce ill-prepared for jobs that require collaboration, innovation, and the ability to solve problems.

Students who struggle with impediments and fail testing protocols will be prone to misbehavior and may be suspended or expelled, or drop out on their own. If the reflections they receive from their teachers are negative or absent, such children will shut down to protect themselves. They protect their vulnerability and sorrow in sheaths of anger or indifference and cease to mature intellectually. This anger and indifference are expressed in various ways as the students become adult citizens; thoughtful questions and discussions are no longer an option. This tragic failure to educate children to become mature citizens with the capacity to develop systems that can be responsibly self-corrected through thoughtful questioning snuffs out our collective hopes for a more just and sustainable world.

Dr. Arthur Costa speaks to the challenge facing all educators:

From an early age, employing a curriculum of fragmentation, competition and reactiveness, students are trained to believe that deep learning means figuring out the truth rather than developing capabilities for effective and thoughtful action. They have been taught to value certainty rather than doubt, to give answers rather than to inquire, to know which choice is correct rather than to explore alternatives.

Our wish is for creative students and people who are eager to learn. That includes the humility of knowing what we don't know, which is the highest form of thinking we will ever learn. Paradoxically, unless you start off with humility, you will never get anywhere, so as the first step you have to already possess that which will eventually be the crowning glory of all learning: the humility to know — and admit — that you don't know and not be afraid to find out.[60]

Michael comes to my mind when I think about creative students asking questions. I can still see him sitting before me, listening intently to whatever I had to say and beginning to formulate his questions about it. Michael was a formidable questioner, taking issue with everything from social mores to philosophical positions, so it didn't surprise me when he came up with an unusual question to research for his senior term paper project. Michael wanted to ascertain what would happen if he stopped using all forms of the personal pronoun for a period of time. I wrote to Michael, who is currently on the faculty of Barrett Honors College at Arizona State University, and asked him what he remembered about this project and whether it had any lasting effect on him:

The immediate inspiration for the project was the writings of Robert Anton Wilson, an occultist, neopagan, conspiracy theorist, and novelist with whom Nathan Sidoli and I were somewhat obsessed at the time. Looking back, Wilson stands for me as a prime example of how you can learn, and grow, and take inspiration from the most unpromising sources.... Although I agree with him on almost nothing at this point, he started me down the road toward my current thinking about witchcraft, and magic, and religion.

Wilson wrote quite a bit about the "general semantics" of Alfred Korzybski — an applied form of linguistic relativism that sought to reform society by changing our speaking practices. In particular, Korzybski sought the abolition of all forms of the verb "to be," which he thought was used in a lazy way that promoted category mistakes and in an instrumentalist way that promoted propaganda.... One of his classic examples (I paraphrase from memory) is the phrase "boys will be boys," in which the first "boys" usually denotes some particular boy or group of boys, and the second "boys" denotes stereotypical characteristics of boydom. The phrase thus seems to state the obvious but actually does covert ideological work, excusing some behavior (mischief, sexual harassment, etc.) as a natural expression of a fictive essence. If "to be" is disallowed, you can't say "boys will be boys," but only "this boy has acted in a way that boys often act" — a circumlocution which, arguably (I am no longer persuaded, but take the point), exposes the ideological underpinnings of the first phrase.

Around the same time, I was reading Whorf's **Language, Thought, and Reality,** *the classic statement of linguistic relativism. And somewhere, I can't now remember where, I read a variant of Korzybski advocating the abolition of "I," "me," "mine," "myself," etc. to rewire one's thinking in a less egotistical direction. That formed the basis of the thesis: to go without those words for a week and chronicle the experiential results.*

I don't remember what I wrote. I do remember that the overall effect was the opposite of what was intended: trying to avoid these words made me notice them and think about them all the time so that I focused on myself and my speech habits. In a roundabout way, this may have had the intended effect, making me aware of just how ego-centered I was — in something of the same way that a fast can make one aware of how unconsciously central food is to one's habits.

Although I now don't think I learned much directly from the thesis, the experience certainly did influence me. My interest in linguistic relativism carried over into college and shaped much of my choice of classes in linguistics and anthropology, which eventually led toward my current work on witchcraft and magic. The uninformed scorn for and dismissal of linguistic relativism I found in my readings of current anthropology (it was thoroughly out of fashion in the 90s) honed my critical faculties and shaped my long-standing suspicion of scientism and reductionism — a suspicion central to nearly all of my recent work, which tends to argue against neurobiological and evolutionary-psychological approaches to religion and magic. More personally, the experiment confirmed for me that thought and speech are intertwined so that how you talk shapes who you are. After years of living in a hyper-intellectualized way given over fully to the academy, I've recently been working on myself and my own speech habits in ways meant to deprogram some of my habits and predispositions. In particular, I've been working on my tendency to "mansplain" so as to make conscious to myself — and to change — my habits of patriarchal domination.

Michael's writing speaks for itself. I intended to edit his response and then discovered how difficult it was to do that. Michael responded fully to my question by demonstrating how he followed his own line of questioning. He is still honing his critical faculties and "deprogramming" himself, as deeply committed to his free agency and questions as he was when I first met him over twenty-five years ago. I also note that a number of my senior students chose thesis topics that later became directions for them in college and life.

Michael is a creative thinker, a teacher who lives with and through the questions that he asks himself. He is willing to live with the questions that do not have easy answers, the questions that probe the nature of reality, life as we know and experience it, and the mystery of our "selves." He reminds me of the moments I stood with my students in the face of this mystery, struck silent by wonder and surprise. In such moments, we are united by our deepest questions—the ones to which our lives as lived may be the only answer. In the face of these existential questions, my age and experience did not give me an edge. I could not answer the questions asked in the following poem, but I could claim them as my own.

WHAT IS AN OCEAN?
Wind singer, night prowler,
Fire eater, water walker,
Earth seer, Time wanderer,
*   God server,*
What are these but dreams?
Images? For this one moment in time,
Just this one moment, please wonder:
*   What are these words?*
*   How did they come?*
For this one very moment, please
*   Think what is an ocean?*
*   What is fire? And please,*
*   Tell me, what is poetry*
But words? What is Ocean
*   But water? What is fire*
*   But heat?*
*   Now wake up!*
*   You have fallen asleep in a*
*   bed of Dream, and now tell me*
*   What are you?*

—**Nate**, age ten

EXPLORE QUESTIONS WITH YOUR STUDENTS

1. **Ask your students real questions.** Real questions do not have fixed or "check the right box" answers. Real questions are open ended and stimulate thought by examining different perspectives, possibilities, and known evidence.

   We learn and make discoveries through this process, through not being satisfied with pat answers, through continuing to question our conclusions and challenge conventional wisdom. Yet our textbooks and testing protocols often teach children the opposite: that there are "right" answers that deserve no further questioning. Bringing a questioning mind to a multiple-choice test can be a liability that slows progress and lowers scores.

   Each day offers teachers multiple opportunities to be models. "Is that true?" is a question that helps us sort through the floods of information from our digital and print sources as well as the stories we tell ourselves about ourselves and the world around us.

   This question is particularly pertinent for children who are learning to use internet sources to find information. Our educational system has failed the citizens who applaud liars who support their prejudices rather than thoughtful leaders who might challenge their ideas and guide them wisely through this perilous time.

2. **Check out these excellent programs that help teachers and students become thoughtful questioners.**

   Marilee Adams, founder of Inquiry Institute, offers multiple suggestions. Here is a sample:

   The questions on the Top 12 List evolved out of Marilee Adams's work with coaching clients and workshop participants over many years. The list can be used in at least three ways: First, it is a logical sequence of questions to help you work through any situation you might want to change or improve. Second, you might just want to scan the list for questions you've been missing. Third, you can turn to it when you're looking for just the right question to emphasize in a particular situation.

Within this list are questions that are applicable to a variety of life's challenges. The goal is to integrate these questions into your everyday thinking. Then, when a challenge arises, you'll be able to easily recall some of them. Not every question applies to every situation. That's why you'll want to develop a collection of your favorites and work with them on a regular basis. These questions can open and change your mind. They allow you to unveil new choices, options, and possibilities you might otherwise have missed.

Here's the list:

- *What do I want?*
- *What are my choices?*
- *What assumptions am I making?*
- *What am I responsible for?*
- *How else can I think about this?*
- *What is the other person thinking, feeling, needing, and wanting?*
- *What am I missing or avoiding?*
- *What can I learn?*
  from this person or situation?
  from this mistake or failure?
  from this success?
- *What action steps make the most sense?*
- *What questions should I ask (myself or others?)*
- *How can I turn this into a win-win?*
- *What is possible?*

Keep this list in a handy place where you can refer to it whenever you feel stuck, want new alternatives, or a change.[61]

Professor Arthur Costa's Institute for Habits of Mind offers free materials, books, videos, and principles for thoughtful inquiry.[62] His website, TeachThought: We Grow Teachers, develops his principles and trains teachers on how to embody the practices in their classrooms.[63]

Problem-based learning and project-based learning provide a rich opportunity for students to deepen their knowledge, expand their repertoire of technical skills, and enhance their appreciation of thinking tools, processes, and strategies.

It is not enough, however, to understand concepts and principles and to solve that one problem, as challenging as it might be. The essential outcome is to develop and expand the dispositions of skillful problem solvers who can apply their learnings to an ever-expanding array of challenges not only in commonly taught subjects in school, but also in their communities, in their world, and their lives.

While we are interested in how many answers individuals know, we are even more interested in how they behave when they don't know — when they are confronted with life's problems the answers to which are not immediately known. The larger goal is for enhanced performance under challenging conditions that demand strategic reasoning, insightfulness, perseverance, creativity, and craftsmanship to resolve complex problems. Achieving this vision requires the internalization of certain dispositions, propensities, or habits of mind.[64]

For Parents: Take your children's questions seriously. If you don't have an answer, research together. Use the sources listed here to deepen your inquiry skills. Don't be afraid to admit when you have been wrong, and share what you are learning with your children. Your interest in your child's questions and your honesty and humility about your own perspectives are a powerful model for creative inquiry and build mutual respect.

. . . . .

I was not aware of these sources during my years as a teacher. Reading through them now inspires me and makes me wish I could do it all over again. Dr. Costa and colleagues also reassure me that I was on the right path with my students when I encouraged their questions and challenged them to think about what they were learning.

Developing and expanding our individual and collective capacities as skillful questioners and problem solvers is an imperative necessity, given the existential problems that are currently threatening our quality of life, perhaps even our survival. We need people with these skills to become leaders who can support such inquiry and turn it into constructive action.

Chapter Nine

We Learn by Doing

We learn by going where we have to go.
— **Theodore Roethke,** *The Waking*

I have an amazing opportunity here to learn great things and to help the world through the knowledge I have.
— **Cole Duckwall,** age twelve

Asking questions that don't have easy answers leads to examining what we have experienced in the past, paying attention to what we are experiencing in the present, and planning for future actions. Questioning and learning through experience are intrinsically connected parts of the same process and are primary to natural learning. We learn what to do and how to do it through our successes, and we learn what not to do by suffering the consequences of our mistakes.

When we are learning through experience, we are not only collecting important information, but we are also developing capacities. I learned about the importance of engaging the natural ways that children learn through my experience in the classroom as I tried and observed various approaches to teaching over many years. John Holt may have initially alerted me to the issue, but my experience is what shaped my teaching style and now motivates me to write about what I learned.

We learn best through experience, by doing and by imitating. This is how we learned through the millennia how to hunt, farm, know which plants we could eat, build shelters, and survive harsh winters. This is also how we learn to communicate with each other. When my grandson was eight years old, he asked his mother how people came to communicate by making noises, how language came to be, how we know, for example, that saying "shoe" is a symbol for a shoe. Simply pondering that question for a moment gives us a glimpse into ourselves, into what it means to be a human being with this amazing but always challenging capacity for communication through language and the complexity of the process by which we come to understand and connect with a constantly changing world around us.

From that perspective, I can see the dynamic tension between "this is what we need to know" and "this is how we do it" and the discovery of new information, insights, and questions that lead us beyond the known. History, both personal and cultural, is the story of this dialectic, how discovery upsets conventional systems of power and belief, how consciousness changes through time in response to new information and experience. This dynamic tension should animate our educational systems and every classroom. A teacher who asks good questions and is responsive to the questions that are living in her students is modeling how to do that. Far more important than the answers that come as a result of the inquiry is the growing ability of the students to ask these questions and to know what they need to do to come to possible answers as they learn through experience.

This approach works for all subjects, even history, which is usually taught through textbooks and lectures. I told my sophomore class a number of iconic stories about the ancient Greeks, building a contrast between militaristic Sparta and democratic Athens. To have a feeling for what an extraordinary moment this was in the development of human consciousness, we divided the class into teams of two students and assigned each team a pre-Socratic philosopher to research around the theme "What is the nature of reality?" We scheduled a two-hour class for a presentation and debate about their findings. The students wore brightly colored togas over their jeans and stood proudly to role-play their philosophers and present their core assumptions and principles to the group.

After the initial presentations, we had a Greek-style free-for-all debate with the understanding that the winners would be the best orators, the ones capable of presenting the strongest and most effective argument, effectively silencing everyone else. Bedlam ensued, and I don't remember which philosopher won, but the value of this experience became evident in the following weeks when I realized that some of the students were spending their lunch breaks creating Socratic dialogues. *Don't interrupt us; we're doing philosophy!* I could see that the developmental capacities awakening in these fifteen- to sixteen-year-olds had found a good match in those ancient Athenians.

My teachers instructed me to memorize math facts and logarithms as an elementary student. They did not encourage me to think mathematically or require me to use mathematics to answer real questions and find possible solutions. Programmed to plug in a pattern that would give me the "right" answer, I struggled in algebra because I didn't understand what the algebraic equations were for or why I would ever need to use them. In the process, I developed a math anxiety that further impeded my abilities. I learned from this experience that I wasn't good at math. The failure of my teachers to recognize why I was struggling and to help me overcome this impediment led me to avoid math once I had passed the basic requirements in high school and college. This situation persisted until I, in turn, had to teach basic math concepts and procedures.

I was fortunate to find Marilyn Burns's hands-on website, Math Solutions, which showed me how to transform my early experience and provide a more experiential, problem-solving approach for my students.[65] Instead of dittoed math sheets, my second graders came into a room with six tables, each with a sheet of challenges and sets of manipulatives they could use to solve them. Each group charted their answers collaboratively, asking further questions and trying out answers before moving on to the next table. I observed a noticeable increase in enthusiasm for math and a decrease in anxiety and stress.

In third grade, my students learned measurement by cooking (teaspoons, pints, cups, quarts, etc.) and building a hexagonal deck for our school garden. Working again in teams, they had to measure (inches, feet, yards) and cut very exactly. Having usable products—a delicious Thanksgiving dinner cooked for parents, a beautiful deck they could all sit on as a group—gave their learning purpose and meaning.

Viola Spolin's improvisation exercises led me down a new path in relation to my training in theater. I was challenged by the process of bringing a play to life, learning to move beyond memorized lines and movements by working with my fellow actors to create an experience for an audience, but this creativity was expressed within necessarily strict parameters. What I had to do and say was given. To step in front of an audience without such givens and be called on to create an experience in the moment was terrifying but also exhilarating when it worked. Improvisational theater is a team effort. What I do affects what you do. Together, we create a particular space and series of events for an audience to imagine and experience. In turn, the audience can be actively involved, making requests and suggestions that determine the action. The results may not offer the wisdom, the potential for catharsis or transformation that is the hallmark of great theater. But improvisation can be a powerful learning tool, building confidence in our ability to move beyond scripts into a realm in which failure can be hilarious and success unexpected and joyous. My experience with improvisation made me a more confident teacher. "We learn by going where we have to go."

I recognize these values in the writings and curriculum guides of veteran teacher/educator Marion Brady, who also observed that students learn best when they can undertake real-world, hands-on tasks that teach them something that they are interested in knowing. Dr. Brady calls his project-centered approach reality-based learning. If our traditional curriculum offers students "a crossword puzzle with all the blanks filled in," Dr. Brady's approach offers the questions and structure that support students to find their own answers or even make their own puzzles. Instead of passively receiving the informational content of various disconnected courses, students elect a project and begin by researching its past to develop a sound understanding of what needs to happen in the present as well as the future. In a recent *Washington Post* article, Dr. Brady stressed the importance of developing the skill of fostering new knowledge:

My objection [to the Common Core tests] begins with the superficiality of the standards' stated aim — to prepare the young "for college and careers." As H.G. Wells pointed out, civilization is a race between education and catastrophe. Societies — at least the thoughtful ones — educate to survive.

Change — environmental, demographic, technological, institutional, and so on — is inevitable, continuous, and unpredictable. To survive, societies must either control changes or adapt to them, both of which require new knowledge. New knowledge is created by the discovery of relationships between parts of reality not previously thought to be related. For example, as infants, we discover a relationship between crying and getting attention. Most adults discover a relationship between personal autonomy and job satisfaction. Societies discover (or don't) a relationship between differing societal cognitive systems and misunderstanding and conflict.

Maximizing the relationship discovery process — not mentally storing secondhand information — is Education Job One.

Reality is complex, which makes the 1893 core curriculum appealing. Specialized study — breaking knowledge apart and creating a school subject to study each part has a long and impressive history of yielding benefits. But ignoring reality's holistic, systemically integrated nature and the seamless way our minds make sense of it comes at a huge, even deadly cost. We're poorly equipped to make sense of the big picture, the trends of the era, and the unintended consequences of our actions because we literally can't imagine possible, probable, and preferable futures. We can't imagine alternative futures because they're products of complex dynamic, systemic interactions, and a curriculum that compartmentalizes knowledge — as the core curriculum does — blocks the basic relating process that imagining requires.

The Common Core State Standards didn't just stop the effort in the 1980s to explore the knowledge-integrating potential of General Systems Theory as it developed during World War II. It locked the fragmented 1893 curriculum — the curriculum I believe is the major reason academic performance has flat-lined for decades — in an even more rigid place.

If we care about the future, the core curriculum can't take us where we need to go. Don't take my word for it. I'm merely saying what well-known and respected scholars have been saying for many years.[66]

Waldorf schools generally follow a subject-based curriculum in which teachers have a great deal of freedom in how they choose to approach and develop each topic. If I could make my own school program, I would shift the primary focus from subjects to issues, particularly in high school, from what we know to what we don't know. We could take global warming as our topic — a reality that is impacting and threatening our future — and investigate multiple issues and paths of action. We could investigate what is actually going on in the soil, for example, and then document how our ignorance of something as basic as the complex nature of the carbon cycle has led to many inventions and interventions that have further depleted our soil instead of restoring it. We could explore situations in which scientists have solved specific problems only to find out down the road that they have created a whole new set of problems from the solution. I would tell them the story of how my uncle, former head of the Botany Department at UC Davis, believed that he was literally saving the world when he helped to develop DDT. Then we might read *Silent Spring*.

Using this template—understanding the largest possible systemic web of relationships and effects—as a lens, we could examine any number of current practices. We might look at the process of patenting genetically modified seeds, for example, and examine the potential physical, economic, and social consequences of this innovation, making a risk/benefit analysis and deciding whether such activity is necessary or morally wrong. Or we could examine our current medical-pharmaceutical model that has resulted in serious inequities with profit margins on drugs trumping safety and public health.

In middle school, we could focus on issues in our immediate community. We could look at the energy profile of our school and propose ways that it could be transformed and improved. We could investigate zero waste management and do surveys in our neighborhoods to see how waste is being processed. Potential subjects of immediate importance are all around us. Most important are the questions for which we don't have ready answers. Investigating, researching, and following the questions that emerge from a circle of engaged students could determine their courses of study. This is very different from following a set subject curriculum that relies heavily on teacher presentation. Again, the primary goal of project-based inquiry is the development of capacities beyond, but not in any way excluding, the ongoing acquisition of information and knowledge.

I visited Michael Becker's classroom at Hood River Middle School in Hood River, Oregon, and witnessed how transformative such a project-based approach can be. Michael used a permaculture model to lead his middle school science students in building an outdoor classroom by creating a food forest on bare, shady ground adjacent to the school buildings. In subsequent years, he spearheaded building a zero-waste-and-energy music and science wing for the school. Students were involved with architects and engineers at every step of the process, building systems that would catch and recycle water and generate electrical and heating needs. They built a passive solar greenhouse with an aquaculture system for year-round food production. The students manage this process along with an outdoor perennial foodscape and garden. They sell their crops at a local farmer's market.

Michael's junior high students are researchers, engineers, designers, builders, and users immersed in a multi-disciplinary, multi-sensory learning experience. They are engaged in learning at a much deeper and wider level than the learning objectives mandated for their grade. They constantly observe and come to conclusions from their hands-on experiences and collaborations with a community of experts and volunteers.

When I asked Michael what happened when his students graduated to high school, he told me that the high school science programs had to revamp their courses of study to meet them. Dissatisfied with traditional science lessons, the students presented their teachers with proposals for independent, project-based inquiry.

Michael's program embodies the essential aspects of an optimal learning situation: a strong attachment relationship built on mutual respect between teacher and students; experiential learning through hands-on observation and problem solving; group-based inquiry; and interdisciplinary perspectives combining science, mathematics, engineering, design, economics, public relations, communication skills, and community building. The children who graduate from these classes are prepared to understand and respond to the challenges they will face as young adults.

I interviewed several of these future heroes during my visit to the classroom. My interview began with two sixth-grade boys, Aiden Cross and Joe Reitz, who helped me find and use the voice recorder app on my relatively new Android phone. I asked them how their classes with Mr. Becker were different from their other school experiences, and Aiden told me:

> *You get to see things and not just hear about them. It's much more hands on. In other schools, they talk to you and show you*

things on paper. But here, when I take a test, I can actually see in my mind what it [the answer] is because I have done it myself.

Joe told me that the FACS program lets him be outside more:

Being outside, I feel freer and like I have more choices. When you are inside, you have to do this or that, or you have to be on the paper, and everything is all scheduled. Outside, you get to see more, experience more. You get to look at that tree over there and see for yourself all the ways that tree is different now than it was.

When I asked the boys about Mr. Becker's style of teaching, Aidan answered:

Instead of doing everything on paper, he likes to go outside and show us what to do with his hands. He's freer. He lets us make some choices. Like, when we are cooking with him, he tells us what basic ingredients we need, but we decide whether we will cook it dark or cook it light or put chocolate chips and other stuff in it. He lets you learn things by yourself. And then you remember them, and you know them more when you learn by yourself. It's way easier to learn things and to remember and use things when you learn them by yourself.

Joe told me:

In this program, we're learning a lot about learning. Applied math is learning to use the math outside the school program. You get to measure the fish tanks when you put in new fish. You have to figure how much waste they will make. If each tank is two hundred gallons, then how much more water will you have to put in to keep it good for all the fish? Instead of "Darn, I have to go to math," it's "Yay, I get to go to math!"

The next period, I spoke with Emma, an eighth-grade girl who has worked with Mr. Becker's program for several years. She enjoys working with him in the kitchen and garden and problem solving to think about different ways to do things:

A lot of it is guess and check — using our knowledge to see how things work and adjusting to make it more successful. When it's really hands on, you remember it because you have it right in front of you, and you are the one who created it. Hands on means that we are using all five of our senses, making observations, and learning things you can't get out of textbooks. It's a lot more fun, too. It's a process we look forward to. Mr. Becker is great at getting everybody involved, motivated, and actively learning in the process.

Watching Michael and his three-or-more-ring circus full of vibrant, active kids filled me with pleasure and hope for the future. The take-home message is that children are so much more capable than most school programs imagine. When children are not learning, we need to look not only at teachers but at an entire system that has little clue what students can learn and accomplish when given a chance. As Cole Duckwall told me when I asked him what he liked about the FACS program, "I have an amazing opportunity here to learn great things and to help the world through the knowledge I have."

Sitra, the Finnish foundation supporting schools that are equitable communities of inquiry and their published book, *Sustainability, Human Well-Being and the Future of Education,* introduced me to High Tech High, a promising initiative in San Diego that offers answers to how a school system can be structured to support hands-on, collaborative learning.

Developed by a coalition of San Diego civic leaders and educators, High Tech High opened in September 2000 as a small public charter school with plans to serve approximately 450 students. HTH has evolved into an integrated network of sixteen charter schools serving approximately 5,350 students in grades K-12 across four campuses. The HTH organization also includes a comprehensive adult learning environment including a Teacher Credentialing Program and the High Tech High Graduate School of Education, offering professional development opportunities serving national and international educators.

High Tech High is guided by four connected design principles — equity, personalization, authentic work, and collaborative design — that set aspirational goals and create a foundation for understanding our approach.[67]

Robert Riordan and Stacey Cailler describe how these principles have been put into practice in their chapter "Schools as Equitable Communities of Inquiry."[68] These San Diego schools are centers of transdisciplinary inquiry and action in which the questions that are most urgent and shared by a diverse group of students direct the course of study. Teacher-student relationships are collaborative rather than hierarchical, and students move through the day in stable cohorts. Students develop and refine the questions that they decide to pursue. Teachers are trained to be expert facilitators who help students find sources for their research and are themselves participants in a collaborative learning community. The results of their investigations are presented in public presentations and exhibitions and through publications.[69]

Although the guiding voice from the past for this initiative is Paulo Freire,[70] Brazilian educator and philosopher, I recognize many similarities with Steiner's vision for education, with one exception. Freire and the HTH schools that he inspired offer a structure that gets the teacher out of the front of the classroom and allows students to share responsibility for initiating and leading the process of learning. Defining this collaborative role with teachers is a further transformative step towards "trusting children."

Christina was an outstanding student in my tenth-grade history class. But this day, she sat in the back of the room, talking quietly with a friend and paying scant attention to a presentation that I had worked very hard to prepare. I stopped her as she started to leave the room at the end of class and asked her what was up, why she wasn't giving me her attention. She looked at me for a long moment and then asked, "Do you really want to know?"

"Yes," I answered and inwardly braced myself. She said that I was very good at making pictures of what had happened in the past and that she had enjoyed listening to what I had to say, but she was ready now to make her own pictures and ask her own questions. She didn't want me to do it for her anymore, so she didn't listen to my lecture and talked with her friend instead. She apologized for being disruptive, and I thanked her, and she left.

Christina was right, and she was very brave. How many hours of my life had I spent passively receiving information from my teachers without being actively engaged when what I remembered and built on was the work I did myself? How might those hours, days, years of my life and my students' lives have been more productively spent? This is the question that should animate our discussion of education reform. We know how children are most directly engaged in learning. How do we manage, assess, and direct this kind of active learning for large groups of young people in a manner appropriate for their developmental ages? Foregone conclusion: such learning cannot be assessed on multiple-choice, standardized tests. Teaching to the tests by telling the students what they have to memorize and know is anathema to this vital learning process.

I clearly remember my conversation with Christina and can see her standing by the door. I remember the look on her face and in her eyes, as well as her words, but I can't for the life of me remember which course it was I was teaching or what my presentation was about.

INSTEAD OF TELLING CHILDREN
WHAT THEY SHOULD KNOW,
LET THEM FIND OUT FOR THEMSELVES

1. **Let students learn through hands-on, direct experience.** The teacher's role is to design lessons and organize materials so students can investigate, practice, and apply what they are learning in a given subject. Teaching measurement in third grade? Students can cook a meal for their parents, learning about teaspoons, tablespoons, cups, and pints in the process. They can

build something for their classroom or the school, learning how to use a saw and a hammer while mastering concepts such as inches and feet.

Studying basic physics of sound and light? String wires between cans to make "phones" and take them out on the playground. Build or order a shadow lightbox and let students figure out what it teaches them about light. Teach science through experiments and allow students to come to their own conclusions about what they have observed.

The more that students can work on their own and come to their own conclusions, the better they will remember what they have learned. When possible, allow students to make mistakes and then learn from them rather than correcting them and being overly concerned about the right answers. Learning *how* is more important than learning *what*. Homework can give students ideas about projects they can opt to try at home. The only worksheets should be records of what they have done and what they have learned from the activity.

2. **Allow students to participate in teaching by researching and presenting information.** In this way, students practice speaking to groups and presenting what they have learned in a clear and interesting manner. Again, the process is as important as the content. Students will remember what they have presented much better than anything the teacher (or other students) present. They will also learn how to actively engage their classmates.

3. **Investigate system-based learning on Marion Brady's excellent website, which contains free lesson plans and instructional materials.** Here is a sampling of what Brady has to say:

Our brains cannot handle massive amounts of random data, and much of what students are now taught falls into that category. The educational establishment's historical theory of learning is best exemplified by the old saying, "If you throw enough mud on the wall, some of it is bound to stick."

Each day, students are given a few minutes of this and a few minutes of that, with little concern given to how the information fits together logically or to the mind's need for order. That's why we remember so little of what we learned in school.

In the early years of the 20th century, long before the news media explosion and the Internet compounded the problem of information overload, British mathematician, teacher and philosopher Alfred North Whitehead was telling the educational establishment it was flooding students' minds with too much miscellaneous stuff. "Let the main ideas which are introduced into a child's education be few," he said, "and let them be thrown into every combination possible." The educational establishment wasn't listening then. And it isn't listening now. The world we're trying to help young people understand is a single, systemically integrated whole. The curriculum we're using to try to explain that whole to kids is a random, disjointed, fragmented, incoherent mess. We accept it because it's what we're taught. And, because we think we're pretty smart, it must be OK.

It isn't OK. Kids show up for kindergarten with a mental system for organizing and relating information already firmly in place in their minds, a system built into language and culture. That system is far more sophisticated than the educational approach adopted in the 1890s, which gave us the current industry-inspired collection of narrow subjects and courses. We need to make that implicit "natural" system explicit, base general education on it and help students see the whole of which their specialized studies are a part.[71]

4. **Investigate Project-based Learning** (PBL) is a student-centered pedagogy in which students acquire deeper knowledge through active exploration of real-world challenges and problems. The Buck Institute for Education offers training and assistance for teachers and school districts interested in implementing project-based learning programs. They have trained eighty

thousand teachers across fifty states and worked with twelve hundred schools.[72] Michael Becker's classroom at Hood River Middle School, described in this chapter, is an outstanding example of such a program.

5. **Investigate High Tech schools**. Visit, if you can, to see a transformative program for twenty-first-century students in action. I end this chapter with a quote from *Schools as Equitable Communities of Inquiry* by Riordan and Callier:

Public schools, whatever their shortcomings, remain the linchpin of social cohesion — the one place where individuals from all walks of life — rich or poor, urban or rural, male or female, all races and ethnicities, all religions, all sexual orientations, all talents and abilities — come together. As such, schools have a responsibility to serve all students and to serve the greater good, and to pursue questions attendant to those purposes. Even the most equitable schools cannot themselves resolve the large issues we face, but they can model shared vision and collective action. As micro-societies, they can enact personal empowerment, democratic processes, design thinking, an emphasis on production as opposed to mere consumption, a focus on sustainability, connections to community, and the development of human and social capital. Both by example and by their action in the world — and by their determination to sustain and renew themselves as equitable communities of inquiry — they can play a critical role in the transition to a sustainable well-being society.[73]

For Parents: Respect your child's capacity to learn best from experience by providing experiences rather than pat answers to their questions. Allowing children to work with you, in the house, the garden, the community, is the best way to provide experience.

· · · · ·

The children in Michael Becker's classes reported that they learned much more through their hands-on projects and what they did and discovered themselves. They also mentioned how much they valued going outside and observing.

Natural settings enhance the benefits of play and hands-on learning. Our many hikes into the hills around our school offered far more than good exercise for restless children.

Chapter Ten

Natural Learning in the Natural World

PEACE OF WILD THINGS
When despair for the world grows in me
and I wake in the night at the least sound
in fear of what my life and my children's lives may be,
I go and lie down where the wood drake
rests in his beauty on the water, and the great heron feeds.
I come into the peace of wild things
who do not tax their lives with forethought
of grief. I come into the presence of still water.
And I feel above me the day-blind stars
waiting with their light. For a time
I rest in the grace of the world, and am free.
                       —Wendell Berry, *Collected Poems*

My grandmother, Della, rode her horse on a dirt road through thick redwood groves to a one-room school in Little River, a community on California's North Coast. My mother walked several miles from her family farm to the three-room school in the center of Potter Valley, a small farming community in the hills east of Ukiah. I walked two long blocks from my house to my elementary school in Westwood, a lumber company town in the High Sierra. My three grandchildren get into a car every morning and are driven on the freeway to their school in a neighboring town. We need only enter into these three snapshots to sense the profound changes that have brought us to our present moment of ecological crisis and the perception that many of our children may be suffering multiple physical and mental problems as a result of "nature-deficit disorder."

Young Della loved her horse and enjoyed feeling it move beneath her. Safe in the saddle, she was the queen of a wildly beautiful domain, breathing in the sea air, sensing the seasonal changes as she rode miles through the fog, through the sunlight, through the rain to her destination. Her day began and ended with a burst of freedom. Her horse grazed in a pasture next to the schoolyard, waiting to carry her home. When she told me about this, I was envious. I longed to have a horse and live out in the woods. But the woods were only blocks from my house, and my journeys to school and back acquainted me with all kinds of weather as my friends poured out of their houses and met me on the way, throwing snowballs or splashing in puddles and converging on the playground to play games before we were called into our classrooms.

My grandchildren arrive by car in front of their school just in time for the bell and are picked up soon after. They come home, have a snack, and often start on homework. If the day is nice, they may spend time outside doing a garden chore or activity. My son and daughter-in-law do their best to get them outside to work in the garden and to go camping, biking, or to the beach on the weekends. Their teachers believe in getting them outside as much as possible. But their daily routine, common to most of today's children, is profoundly disconnected from nature or any experience of free agency. In some communities, allowing an elementary-age child to walk alone to school or to play in a neighborhood park can result in a visit from child protective services and a possible charge of neglect.

Today's children are being taught that the world (natural and unnatural) is not safe and they can't be trusted to act wisely in it. Little wonder that their attention is drawn instead into a virtual world of images and messages on screens or that children, who are naturally attracted to adventures that test their capacities, are spending an average of thirteen hours a week playing video games instead of exploring the woods or the countryside. Medline reports that most American children spend an average of three hours a day watching TV. All types of screens can total five to seven hours a day.[74] Medical professionals are concerned with health impacts and cite rising rates of childhood obesity with concomitant illnesses: diabetes, heart disease, and cancer.[75]

The impacts on brain and neurological development are less discussed but potentially just as serious. By 2019, 3.3 million children in the United States, roughly five out of every hundred, were taking a prescription medicine for ADHD.[76] A child with ADHD has great difficulty focusing and relaxing physically or being quietly reflective. It is an indictment of our whole culture when so many children are not thriving and maturing in a healthy manner. One obvious remedy might be to shut off those flickering images on the screens and send the children out to play. We might then investigate the role that sunlight, fresh air, and physical activity in a natural setting play in children's healthy development.

Neuroscientist Dr. Regalena "Reggie" Melrose affirms the importance of natural settings in her article "Why Waldorf Works from a Neuroscientific Perspective."

> *According to years of research recently compiled by Dr. Eeva Karjalainen, natural green settings reduce stress, improve mood, reduce anger and aggression, increase overall happiness and even strengthen our immune system.... When we experience nature, our blood pressure, heart rate, muscle tension, and level of stress hormones all decrease faster than when we are in urban settings. In children we know that ADHD symptoms are reduced when they are given the opportunity to play in green settings.[77]*

Scott Sampson, paleontologist and author of *How to Raise a Wild Child*, offers parents and teachers a guide to inspire reconnection and love of nature in all children:

Nature's impacts extend far beyond physical fitness, encompassing intellectual and emotional health, self-identity, and basic values and morals. Health benefits of exposure to nature include enhanced healing, stress reduction, creativity and self-esteem. Nature also has an unparalleled capacity to stir our emotions, fostering raw and powerful feelings of wonder, awe, mystery, joy — and yes, fear. Smelling a wildflower in an alpine meadow, sprinting into the ocean surf, and sharing a face-to-face encounter with a coyote are all experiences that differ mightily from virtual alternatives.[78]

Nature-deficit disorder is now a trending concern. A back-to-nature movement has mounted campaigns in the U.S. and six other countries, led by groups such as The Children & Nature Network, co-founded by Richard Louv, author of *Last Child in the Woods*.[79] Children, however, are not the only ones suffering from this disorder. How many people leave home in the dark to work all day in an artificially lit building, only to return home in the dark again? The profound impact on our collective soul life of this disconnection from the natural world is described poignantly by Jungian therapist Frances Weller in *The Wild Edge of Sorrow*:

We are born, as psychiatrist R.D. Laing reminds us, "as Stone Age children." Our entire psychic, physical, emotional and spiritual makeup was shaped in the long evolutionary sweep of our species. Our inheritance includes an intimate and permeable exchange with the wild world. It is what our minds and bodies expect. Eco-psychologist Chellis Glendinning calls this original enfoldment in the natural world the primal matrix. We were embedded in this matrix of life and knew the world and ourselves only through this perception. It was an unmediated intimacy with the living world, with no trace of separation between the human and the more-than-human world.

What was once a seamless embrace has now become a breach, a tear in our sense of belonging. Glendinning calls this our original trauma. This trauma carries with it all the recognizable symptoms associated with psychic injury: chronic anxiety, dissociation, distrust, hypervigilance, disconnection and many others. We are left with a profound loneliness and isolation that we rarely acknowledge. It is as if we have completely normalized our condition.

And yet, this feeling of separation profoundly affects the range of our reach, the ways we participate in the landscape and sense our allegiance with the living world. Our soul life flickers dimly, and rather than feeling a kinship with the entire, breathing world, we inhabit and defend a small shell of a world, occupying our daily life with what linguist David Hinton calls the "relentless industry of self." [80]

Only a profound disconnect from the natural world and our fellow humans allows us to continue pillaging the earth and seeing its life systems as resources without responsible awareness or accountability for the consequences of our actions. The extreme individualism behind the drive to build a world economy based on endless growth through the use of non-renewable resources is not responsible or sane. But corporate leaders, who insulate themselves from the impacts of their decisions and justify their actions in terms of wealth creation, are currently in power around the world. They dominate all cultural and political sectors of our global societies, including our educational systems, hence the campaign to remove education from the public sphere and privatize schools, i.e., make a profit while influencing the content of the curriculum. We must stop normalizing such behavior and begin to hold these oligarchs and the politicians they've purchased accountable. We are all deeply, inextricably connected and affected by every change they have made. We can only ignore the damage and try to cut ourselves out of the equation for so long before such avoidance teaches everyone, including them, harsh lessons.

We need a profound shift, not only in what we do and in how we live but also in how we see ourselves in relationship to the natural world and to each other. This shift must become a central mission in the way we educate children and re-educate ourselves. Children must learn that they are an inextricable part of the natural world, not on computer screens or in zoos but in what is left of the wild. We must learn with them and from them how to reconnect and begin to understand our true place in this magnificent evolutionary journey called life. Our most important learning will begin with unlearning and looking with fresh eyes, asking questions, and listening carefully to the answers to go beyond the conditioned assumptions that promote ignorance.

Witnessing my struggle to connect with first graders after many years of teaching high school students, a wise mentor told me that the world I had to re-enter was not a world of cute imaginary gnomes and fairies but of possibility in which, at any moment, one might encounter the real thing.

Remembering was just that, re-membering, feeling in my feet, legs, hands, and arms, in my body and not in my head, how it feels to be a young child who lives fully in the present moment as a physical being. I took the children on frequent walks to a local park with a creek, where we took off our shoes and got our feet wet. We hiked all over the wooded hills near our school and went on day hikes to special places like Muir Woods. Each expedition brought back treasures for our nature table, a rich trove of unusual rocks, cocoons, bones, snake skins, bugs, and the like, raw material for stories, drawing, and beeswax sculptures.

I wrote a series of stories for the children when they were in second grade called *Mother Oak* about the creatures that depend on an old oak tree and each other for life. I wanted the stories to give the children an introduction to systems ecology as it manifests in our oak woodland biome. On our hikes, the children looked for and tried to identify the animals: Eddie Squirrel, Bertha Beetle, Sassy Jay, Mother Deer, Sally Salamander, Geordi Fox, and Dusty Woodrat (identified by his big nests high in the oak trees). The story also described the fates of a cluster of acorns, separated from Mother Oak by a sudden storm. We gathered acorns on one hike, sprouted them on a classroom windowsill, and then planted them along our path up the mountain, marking the sites with small flags. Over the months that followed, we checked to see which acorns had survived and were beginning to grow. We talked about the Native Americans who had hunted there and gathered the acorns for food. The students' first writing assignments were to retell these stories in their own words. At the end of the series, I wrote out the stories by hand, and one of the mothers in our class drew illustrations. I gave each child a book to keep that we used to practice reading cursive writing.

Through this two-year process of immersion in nature and stories about nature, I became aware that something profound was happening to me. In the spring of that year, I gave a talk at the Healthy Schools Conference in Fair Oaks, California, about my experience as a teacher of young children. I ended by saying:

At moments, I am able to find my way back, down the long years to something I can't name. When that happens, there is a quiet, a lively peace that comes over the class and flows through the rest of our day together. They look at me differently then, and I feel seen all the way down. When I am less than fully present, fixed in my agenda or my smile, they let me know that, too. Every day, I feel such gratitude that I have been given this opportunity for healing, for making whole, for recovering myself. There is nothing I would rather do than make this journey through the grades with these companions. I wish I could still have tea with my friend, M. C. Richards, who started me on this quest and who has now crossed the threshold ahead of me. I would speak to her these words from her poem, "Recovery of the Child in Adulthood": "The child who wept and who weeps still I take in my arms for its tears are alive and carry life out my eyes, down my cheeks, down the cracks of the earth for the yield." [81]

Nature studies were woven through each year that I taught this group of children, first as stories and outdoor activities and later as systems ecology and science. My class spent several hours a week working in the school garden. At the end of the second grade, the children sowed a bed of wheat. In the fall of the third grade, we reaped the wheat, ground it into flour, and then baked bread for everyone to share. We cooked all year, bringing vegetables in from the garden to turn into soup and snacks for the class. We studied the Miwok, Pomo, and Ohlone tribes in the fourth grade and tried to imagine what their lives were like in the little valley that now held our school. We spent several days at Fort Ross, up the California coast, cooking outside on an open fire and sleeping on the floor in the old wooden barracks of this early Russian outpost.

In fifth grade, the children learned about photosynthesis and plants, observing, drawing, and painting, watching what happens as plants grow, flowers bloom, and blossoms fade. We hiked in each season to a beautiful spot in the hills that James had discovered. Each student found a special place to sit in silence, writing down observations. We returned to this spot several times during the year to record the changes wrought by the seasons. In the spring, we took our studies into the woods with a local herbalist and spent a week on California's Lost Coast, camping, hiking, swimming, and learning about local flora. We also spent time at the San Francisco Zen Center's farm and retreat center near Muir Beach, combining our study of botany with learning about Buddha and practicing meditation.

Throughout all of these years, we hiked, camped, and participated in environmental outdoor programs, sometimes overnight but often for a week at a time. We spent a week camping and working on a biodynamic farm that used Percheron horses to pull its plows. We studied volcanoes in Mt. Lassen Park, glacial action in Yosemite, and gold mining in the California foothills. We watched elephant seals mating in a downpour at Año Nuevo and kayaked in Monterey Bay. We hiked portions of California's Lost Coast and swam in wet suits off the waters of Catalina Island, looking down into the kelp beds for sharks.

These outings are what my graduating eighth graders remembered best when I asked them what they had learned. They spoke of the nights around the campfire after climbing a mountain or hiking along the ocean, of lying on our backs in a mountain meadow, identifying constellations in the myriad stars above us, of swimming in a pristine swimming hole surrounded by sunning rocks or sleeping in a circle on the beach and being invaded by raccoons. These are my precious memories, too, worth all of the effort that it took to make them happen safely. At graduation, my students shared what they remembered about going through the grades. Here are some of those short speeches:

We walked down the scraggly cliff to the crashing waves on the beach. Kaya, Theron, Jasper, Allison and I were the hunters who had to find food — in this case, fish — so our tribe could eat dinner. We climbed onto a big, flat rock and put our lines into the water and waited, and waited, and waited. Not even a nibble. We had to go back to the fort empty handed! We zigzagged to the top and trudged after Richard Jenkins, who surprised us by taking a turn into the parking lot. In the back of Mike Watt's gray van was a cooler, and in that cooler was a big, gutted salmon. We put that fish in our net, plastered big smiles on our faces, and walked proudly back to camp, successful hunters at last.

—**Kinzie,** remembering the trip to Fort Ross
at the beginning of fourth grade

I sat in awe of the destruction and disappearance of nature caused by the hydraulic miner's urgent search for gold. Despite being appropriately dressed as if we were one of them, my mind could not imagine life in the now-deserted town of Bloomfield with everyone caught up in gold fever and going to the Diggins, caring not a bit for the beauty of the world around them.

—**Annamalka,** remembering our week-long
fourth-grade trip through the Gold Country

Several massive rocks lay in a clump on the hillside above Lucas Valley. They sat there, covered in thick moss and the swaying shadows of buckeye and oak, partially submerged in the dirt that had surrounded them for eons. The wind in the trees overhead and the sound of a gurgling stream were the only sounds that penetrated the vast silence created between their dappled faces. We sat there, reposing in various places around them, just taking in the world and trying to write poems. For some, the inspiration was there, and the words flowed with ease onto the paper. For others, the words refused to come until they saw a special tree, or leaf, or stone, and then the poem came, fast as the wind that blew. And, as always, there were those like me who couldn't find the words or the inspiration at all. We sat there for what seemed like hours but, in reality, was only fifteen minutes until Mrs. Cummings called us over and we began our descent down the hill. I have been back there hundreds of times since and have still to find the words to describe the serenity and peace that emanates from that place. And until the day I do, it will remain an unfinished chapter of my life.

—**James,** remembering our fifth-grade visits
to the hills behind our school

Bumping along a dirt and gravel road along the Lost Coast, our class was wondering what Ms. C. had in mind. There was no civilization at all. We came to a dead end and all got out of the cars. The sun was shining at its hottest point, and we were all extremely hot. Hidden in some bushes was the beginning of a little trail. We started to hike down, and it got so steep that Justin had to tie a long rope to a tree, and we all held on to it so that we wouldn't fall. When we finally got to the bottom, there was a beautiful water hole. It seemed as if it were untouched by anything but nature itself. The class all jumped off of big rocks into the pool of clear, fresh water, splashing and playing. The boys caught newts and chased some of the girls with them. It was a very magical place, with no one but us, that we had found in the depths of the Lost Coast.

—**Meleah,** remembering our fifth-grade camping trip
to the Lost Coast in Northern California

The hike up Silver Peak is not an easy one. It is more than eight miles long, approximately eighteen hundred feet high, the third-highest point on the island of Catalina, and we hiked it. The way up the mountain is mainly all steep uphill, and the way down is a steep decline. The hike was long, hot, dusty and made me constantly yearn for water, but once I made it to the top, it was one of the most exhilarating and accomplished feelings in the world when I looked down at the clouds and the sea, for I had just hiked through clouds to reach a goal I couldn't even see when I started.

—**Lily R.,** remembering our eighth-grade trip
to Catalina Island

Fifth graders wrote these poems after visiting Muir Beach, San Francisco Zen Center's Green Gulch Farm, and receiving meditation instruction in the zendo.

Light like wind sweeping across the golden wheat plains,
Clouds rushing across the sky and for one moment
Blocking the rays of the golden sun and its warmth.
When bell tones from an unknown distant realm.
Like a bird flying down down and splash landing in a lake
Jolted my senses back to consciousness.

—**Michael B.**

Waves, crashing like stallions on the golden sand,
Ferociously pounding the land,
Trying to go farther, but being reined back by the wind.
Sitting now in the quietness,
Hearing the breath of people around me,
Feeling bare, helpless,
Wrapped up in the extremes
Of good and evil.

—**Genny**

An elf with pointed ears, and her eyes shining
Looked up at me from the garden row,
Her hair was tangled in dreadlocks
And her mouth turned up in a smile from ear to ear
While she dug a hole for the dahlia.

—Linnea

I was aided immeasurably by the Waldorf curriculum's wise and developmentally appropriate process for teaching children about nature. From imaginative immersion in the early years through observation-based science in the middle and high school years, learning is experiential and direct. There are no textbooks. The children draw what they see, tell stories of their experiences, and come to their own conclusions. Engaging in this process of discovery is primary, deemed far more important than memorization and regurgitation of facts and formulas. In high school, this approach weaves intellectual understanding and critical thinking into a strong base of physical and emotional experience gained in the elementary grades. The result is the development of a new capacity in the students: an ethical sense of purpose. When this arises, we know that learning has gone deep enough to inform and give purpose to action.

When the deadliest tsunami in recorded history struck Indonesia in 2004, some of the students in our seventh-grade class felt strongly that they should do something to help. Led by Annamalka and Max, they decided to start a business making healthy snacks to sell after school. The whole class participated in baking and selling shifts, and within a few months, they had collected $3,500, which they sent to tsunami relief. I had nothing to do with organizing this effort besides granting my approval.

When children who have formed strong emotional attachments to the natural world understand as young adults that what they love is in peril, they are moved to do whatever is necessary to protect and restore the beloved. Such young people are rightly feared by those who would prefer to see them conditioned to be an obedient labor force addicted to material consumption.

Coming generations will either struggle desperately to survive or be strongly engaged in creating a more sustainable and just paradigm. Probably both. We do not have any simple answers for them, but I believe in their resilience and creativity if they are given the right opportunities by an education that supports their wholeness of mind, body, and heart, an education that helps them develop a sense of beauty, truth, and goodness from their deep connection with the natural world.

Ami's seventh birthday happened just before her first day of school in our first-grade classroom. We celebrated her birthday after lunch, and Ami and her mother told us the following story.

On her birthday, Ami woke up her mother and told her that she had had an important dream and she wanted to tell her all about it. In her dream, Ami was in a garden, looking at the flowers with a guide. The guide led her to one beautiful flower that seemed to beckon to her, and she found herself becoming small enough to dive down through the blossom into the ground.

The guide then led her deep into the earth to the Great Goddess of All Living Beings, who sat on her throne, surrounded by crystals. This beautiful Queen, the color of dirt, seemed enormous, and the guide told Ami that she was large because of all the love in her heart.

The Queen welcomed Ami and allowed her to hold and play with the lovely fat baby she held in her arms. She told Ami that she had called her and was very pleased that Ami could hear the call. She encouraged Ami to explore her kingdom. Ami gave her the baby and went down a path leading to a fairytale castle. Inside were all the characters from the fairy tales, and she played and danced with the kings, queens, princes, and princesses until the guide told her it was time to return.

The Dark Queen then told Ami that she wanted to show her something, and Ami looked and saw grown-up human beings walking around. But when they got close to the Queen, they averted their eyes, turned, and hurried away.

"Why can't they see you?" Ami wondered, and the Queen answered that they couldn't see her because their hearts had become closed, and they experienced the brightness of her love as pain.

"You can see me, Ami, because your heart is open and pure. Now I have a task for you. I want you to tell your mother about your dream, and when you go to your new school, I want you to tell all the children in your class and your teacher that I am here. That I have always been here and that I love them."

Ami and her mother told the class this story and gave each of us a small crystal as a gift from Ami and the Great Goddess of All Living Beings.

MAKE THE NATURAL WORLD YOUR CLASSROOM

1. Establish a school garden. Students can help build and maintain gardens as well as plant and harvest crops, providing an excellent opportunity for learning through doing. The cycle of composting waste, regenerating soil, and growing and eating organic plants is the best way for students to learn about the natural systems that support life on this planet. Through caring for their gardens, they learn to respect and nurture life systems. They also learn how to curtail the human activities that are currently threatening these systems and their futures. This is perhaps the most important subject we can teach this generation of children, ensuring that they deeply understand what needs to be changed.

    School gardens also build community as students, teachers, and parents who are passionate about gardening come together to work and share information and the fruits of their labors. Resources and garden grants will vary from state to state. Here are some basic websites: the National School Garden Network at farmtoschool.org and How to Start a School Garden at fix. com. These websites list the various benefits of gardening for student health, eating habits, and physical exercise, as well as responsible citizenship. Hire a full-time or part-time garden teacher to oversee the program if possible.

2. **Take students camping.** As an avid camper, hiker, and explorer, I enjoyed planning and leading outdoor adventures, and I had parents who supported this kind of learning and were able to volunteer. Planning such events for a large group of students is challenging. I made detailed arrangements and visited all sites in the summer before each school year. Our class fundraised to support our trips, and parents contributed what they were able to afford. Many parents arranged their schedules for the year so they could come with us. Not all communities will be able to afford the time or expense for these longer trips. Michael Becker, whose classes I observed at Hood River Middle School, has written an article for Edutopia about Outdoor School, an outdoor learning center he developed for his sixth-grade students.[82] He describes the program and gives detailed tips to teachers. If camping trips are out of reach, be sure to take day trips to parks and natural areas.

3. **Investigate environmental programs in your area that are available to your classes and age groups.** I signed up with Yosemite Institute when I took my students to Yosemite for four days and was impressed with the young adults who ran their programs.[83] California State Parks has a series of environmental living programs that we enrolled in to visit Fort Ross, Malakoff Diggins, and Sutter's Fort.[84] Headwater's Outdoor School at Mt. Shasta offers summer classes and programs focused on survival skills.[85] Such programs also carry insurance to cover possible accidents or mishaps.

4. **Explore the natural world near your school by taking frequent walks and hikes.** Our school was in a developed canyon area surrounded by open hills we could explore and that became an extension of our classroom. A parent volunteer or two can make such excursions acceptable to administration. Most neighborhoods have some access to parks or open space. Going

for a walk in a city neighborhood and recording the birds, plants, animals, and creatures that the children observe is worthwhile. Get the children outdoors in all kinds of weather.

5. **Make a Nature Table** in the early grades and adorn it with treasures collected on hikes: puff balls, snake skins, acorns, bones, special rocks, and surprises.

6. **Invite naturalists, rangers, beekeepers, and bird and animal recovery center volunteers (with their creatures) to come and talk with your classes.**

7. **Show nature films.** Films should not replace actually getting students outside, but they can be a supportive addition, particularly when the weather is cold and stormy in winter. My current favorite is called *Hike the Divide,* photographed and narrated by a young environmental activist, Connor DeVane, who hiked the Continental Divide from Canada to Mexico, filming and interviewing people he met on the way.[86]

For Parents: Grow plants with your children. Plant a garden if you can. Grow tomatoes, basil, and herbs on your patio. Go for hikes on the weekend. Go camping, particularly if you live in the city. Explore the parks in your area. Read your children stories about animals and birds. Generations of children in my family loved the Burgess books. Watch nature films. If your child's teacher is organizing outings, join in whenever possible and take part, providing transportation, food, and moral and financial support. These activities will also be a precious gift to yourself.

· · · · ·

Ami's dream that she shared as a gift to her teacher and classmates guided me through my years with this group of children. The Great Goddess of All Living Beings is everywhere — under our feet, in the water we drink, in the air that we breathe. She can live in our classrooms if we invite her in and celebrate her through our drawings, paintings, and activities. If we open our hearts to her love and claim our status as her children, perhaps humility and gratitude can begin to replace the ignorance and greed that currently drive so many choices in our larger society.

As we come to understand how the natural world works and our possible roles in it as protectors and nurturers, perhaps we can begin to infuse our man-made systems with the indigenous wisdom we have lost in the name of progress. This reconnection must weave through everything we learn and do together, from science that expands our knowledge to the celebrations that honor the life rhythm of the seasons and our lives.

Chapter Eleven

Let's Celebrate

Ritual is the pitch through which the personal and collective voices of our longing and creativity are extended to the unseen dimensions of life, beyond our conscious minds and into the realms of nature and spirit.
— **Francis Weller,** *The Wild Edge of Sorrow*

The children were learning about the Miwok people, who once lived in Lucas Valley, where our school was located. I contacted Lenny Pinola, a local Pomo storyteller and medicine man, to see if he was available to speak with our class of fourth graders. Lenny told me that he had been seriously ill with diabetes and was resting, but he invited us to an event—a healing ceremony to be held at nearby Indian Valley Junior College. The college had been erected on land sacred to local tribes, and this ceremony was a gesture to begin a process of reconciliation with local Native Americans.

We gathered with several hundred people in an open green space in the warm autumn sun. At the appointed time, Lenny, on crutches, came up to the microphone. First, he spoke at length about his illness and how he had come close to death and been faced with losing his gangrenous leg. He wept as he thanked the doctors and nurses who had taken care of him and saved his leg from amputation. It was a long story, and I began to wonder when the healing ceremony would begin.

Then Lenny began to tell a second story, this time about his alcoholic brother, the various interventions that they had tried in order to save him and the final tragic result—a fatal car crash. Sobbing loudly, Lenny described his pain at having to tell his mother that her first son was dead. By this time, I was acutely uncomfortable. Parents were looking at me with raised eyebrows, the children were restless, and one mother suggested that perhaps we should leave. Where was the healing ceremony?

As the story ended and Lenny's sobs subsided, drumming and low chanting began, and the audience was asked to stand in a large circle. I didn't fully realize that we were in the middle of the healing ceremony until Lenny came down from the stage and limped over to face the first few people, tribal members, who demonstrated what our response should be. I can't remember the exact words that we spoke, but I do remember the feeling: *I see you; I feel your pain; I love you; together, we will help you get through this difficult time.* Lenny faced each of us around the circle, including the children, and each exchange ended with an embrace. Lenny told us in closing that this traditional ceremony was held monthly by the members of his tribe. It would last for hours as tribal members brought their griefs, regrets, and disappointments to the circle for release and healing.

What a learning moment for me! I had been embarrassed by what I perceived as Lenny's emotional excess. Instead, I was faced with the implications of my own cultural mandate to "put a good face on things" and keep my problems private. When I talked about the ceremony with the children the next day, I also realized that they were not nearly as conditioned. They were still able to cry and shout to get their feelings out, and they were resilient in their ability to recover once they had received a requisite amount of comforting. But how do we, the grownups, too often reflexively respond?

I can remember my own loving mother telling me at such a moment of angry grief that I shouldn't feel the jealousy I was expressing. Worse, as parents and teachers, we are trained to send upset children away from us to their rooms or outside on the ramp or to the office until they can get control of their feelings again. No wonder we were uncomfortable with Lenny.

This experience also caused me to reflect on how many adults and children are on medications to keep their unreleased emotions and unhealed wounds under control and how many traumatized people are self-medicating with drugs. Deaths from drug overdose and suicide are on a steep rise. Gun violence resulting in tragic loss of life is now epidemic. To address this deep cultural *malaise,* we need more than new gun control laws. We need to reestablish healing rituals within our communities and ensure that everyone has access to such circles of support.

The ancient world, as well as the indigenous cultures that are native to this land, was filled with celebrations and ritual practices that gave meaning to shared experiences and provided safety and emotional support for community members.

I read recently that India once had 365 celebratory rituals, one for each day of the year, most of them involved with growing food and eating. Just as we have become disconnected from the natural world, we have lost this sense of the sacred that was once woven through ordinary daily life. Holidays are primarily experienced as time off from work and are used as opportunities for commercial exploitation.

Industrial agriculture does not honor the earth ceremonially or respect the basic principles of living soil. Supermarkets do not teach our children where food comes from or how to be grateful to the earth or farmers.

Many people who feel upset and confused have nowhere to go with their grief or their isolation and despair. Going shopping at the mall or on the internet, our culture's basic cure-all, is only a temporary fix.

I also do not see much discussion about the role of celebration in our educational institutions. Graduation rites are still held and have a celebrative flavor, but our multicultural public schools, which are not allowed to celebrate particular religious festivals in recognition of the separation of church and state, simply offer spring and winter breaks minus any connective rituals or practices.

Communal festivities are focused primarily on competitive sports, another area for commercial exploitation.

I feel like I am looking down a deep, dark hole as I struggle to understand what has happened to bring us to our current dilemma: the multiple ways in which the society we have created is disconnected from our source — this living web of life we call Earth — just as we have become increasingly disconnected from each other and even from ourselves. This cannot be the legacy that we want to pass on to our children. How can we protect them from this dark, materialistic destiny even as its influence pervades every aspect of their daily lives? It is certainly a daunting challenge.

When I experience such moments of existential angst and dread, I find comfort and courage in the words of farmer, poet, and philosopher Wendell Berry:

> *I see that the life of this place is always emerging beyond expectation or prediction or typicality, that it is unique, given to the world minute by minute, only once, never to be repeated. And this is when I see that this life is a miracle, absolutely worth having, absolutely worth saving. We are alive within mystery, by miracle.*[87]

This is the sensibility that I wished to arouse in myself and my students — the sense that life is a miracle, absolutely worth saving and defending, and that we must participate in life with reverence and gratitude for what we receive. Waldorf education took both tenets very seriously, and this was attractive to me, but my personal transformation took time and a number of experiences, such as the one with Lenny Pinola.

Private Waldorf schools wrap students and teachers in daily and weekly rituals and in celebrations, ceremonies, and festivals that mark the cyclical passages of each year. These celebrations are often connected to the course of study. Third-grade students, who hear Old Testament stories, may celebrate Shabbat on Friday afternoons or participate in a seder led by a parent. Fifth graders celebrate Divali, a festival of light, as they study ancient India and hear stories from the Ramayana. The celebrations add experiential depth to the course content and are not intended to proselytize particular religious beliefs. Both the celebrative matrix and world culture curriculum were new to me when I made the shift from public high school to a private Waldorf school.

I was initially frustrated by what I perceived as too-frequent interruptions to the more serious business of education. I was also overwhelmed by the amount of work and preparation I was facing as a teacher who was always preparing new material as I moved up the grades with a group of children. After my first Michaelmas Festival and Harvest Fair, when I was handed a script for the Christmas play that the faculty performed each year for the children and parents, I had my first and only experience of actually having tears spring out of my eyes onto the paper. Really? You want me to do this, too? Yes.

To do it all without burning out, I had to shift my mindset. Could I do less rigorous intellectual preparation and more active participation without losing the academic edge for the children? What was essential for their education? The practices and celebrations took time, but I began to understand that they were adding a deeper dimension than I had experienced in my education or earlier teaching experience, one in which all the essential factors for learning that I have mentioned — relationship, community, stories, active participation and creation, connection to the natural world — come together. I was also learning to relax and enjoy the process and have more faith in my spontaneous responses to questions and ideas that came from the children or current events. These lessons were often the most satisfying, far beyond any that I might have prepared in advance.

I understand now, looking back, that the verses, meditations, celebrations, and festivals that we practiced provided a balance to the materializing forces of modern media and consumer culture. The celebrations and festivals also connected us with a cultural past and with generations of ancestors who had danced the same dances and sung the same songs.

Just as children learn by repetition, by practicing their times tables or their musical instruments or memorizing their lines in a play, our consistent daily practices provided a strong framework for our studies while strengthening our sense of shared effort. Saying a verse or singing a song in unison does more than help children begin and end their school days with consistent focus and intention. Such practices also underscore that we are in this together, helping each other learn rather than competing as a disparate collection of individuals.

Birthday celebrations recognized the precious value of each child. Summer birthdays in our class were celebrated on the half-birthday during the school year. I wrote birthday verses with a drawing for each child through the lower grades. In the upper grades, I chose poetry from the ancient world, Shakespeare, and modern poets. Once a week, each child stood and recited a birthday verse, learning to speak clearly and confidently in the process.

After thirty-eight such recitations, the children knew each other's verses and poems. Yes, twenty-six sonnets and speeches from Shakespeare and twenty-six ancient and modern poems were painlessly learned by heart. The birthday verses also gave me a way to let the children know that I was striving to see and affirm them.

> *FOR GWEN*
> *I would rather see than be seen.*
> *I would rather hear than be heard.*
> *All that surrounds me I take in*
> *and use to create my own world.*
> *The world I reflect back is true; in pictures, in paintings, in words.*
> *I share my love of the world with you.*
> *See and hear through me and learn.*
> *I am the still point in the eye of the storm.*
> *Though winds swirl around me, I'm centered and warm.*

FOR KAIJA
Behold the acrobat, graceful and strong.
Balance in motion, I dance along.
My step is sure and my hands are steady.
For challenges large my soul is ready.
All that is beautiful gives my heart wings.
All that is true deep within me rings.
I am a bubbling mountain stream.
Under rocks see fishes gleam.

FOR GENEVIEVE
A rosebud bloomed one sunny day.
She wanted to sparkle and dance and play.
To be the loveliest rose in sight
and fill the world with love and light.
"But first you must drink the waters of grief
And seek Father Sun to find relief.
Your roots must go deep," said Mother Earth,
"So your true beauty may come to birth."

In addition to our daily verses and songs, we also said various forms of grace before eating, from Hebrew to ancient Hawaiian to Japanese. My students were particularly fond of the one-word Japanese blessing, spoken with a bow: *Itadakimasu!*

Special days of the year were marked by iconic, whole-school observances. Michaelmas, which comes on September 29, the fall equinox, was new to me. I wrote the following article for our school newsletter in September 2001, when my class was in fourth grade:

When I first learned about Michaelmas, I was moved and gratified. This special day gave a sense of balance to my year and marked the change of the season in a particularly meaningful way. The Being behind this festival — the Archangel Michael — is known throughout many of the world's cultures and spiritual traditions as the Protector of Mankind. Known Biblically as the "Countenance of God," he is the guardian of the Hebrew nation; he is said to have appeared to Mohammed, and he is also known in the East, where the Tibetans call him Mahakal and picture him as a bright being carrying a lighted sword.

In ancient legend, Michael battles with Lucifer, once the brightest of all angels, in his fallen form as a fierce dragon. When Michael prevails and casts Lucifer out of heaven down to earth, time begins. During Michaelmas, we recognize this moment as a continuing challenge. With Michael's help, we ask for courage to face the darkening of the year and the darkness within ourselves and in our world. We ask for his sword of light and truth to be our protection as we struggle against myriad forms of the dragon, within and without.

I wrote these words for the Messenger several years ago. This morning, as I read them again, they have urgent significance. On September 11, 2001, the breath of the dragon scorched our land and our hearts. We are devastated by grief and anger and the wish to confront and vanquish the enemy who committed these heartless acts. But the dragon has disappeared into its lair. Hidden deep in the earth, living invisibly in our midst, the dragon bides its time. We face a terrible dilemma: how to call out and fight this dragon without becoming ourselves infected by its poisonous venom. Oh Michael, in this battle, we will truly need your help, your sword of light and truth, this year of all years!

It is not difficult to see evil in the heartless ideological convictions and acts of terrorists who deliberately sew the dragon's teeth of fear and hatred. Would that they were the only enemy and we could defeat them by simple battle. But the dragon also takes other forms — ethnic cleansing, proliferation of nuclear, chemical and biological weapons, great wealth for the few and great poverty for the many, degradation of the water, air and soil of our precious earth, and a popular culture emphasizing self-centered materialism, to name a few.

We sense within ourselves that all these evils are connected, but the task is overwhelming. Where do we begin?

As we struggle with such questions, and surely such struggle is essential if we are ever to prevail, one thing is clear — that we must, each of us, continually confront the dragon within. We must face the fallen aspects of ourselves: our failure to love or to take responsibility for the consequences of our actions, our tendency to shut down to the needs of others, our prejudices, our greed and our fear. When we confront these fallen tendencies with our higher selves, our honesty, our compassion, our commitment to our families and communities, our willingness to sacrifice for the greater good, our ability to forgive and our humility, the seeds of the dragon will not find fertile soil in our hearts. The light of Michael shines all around us in inspiring stories of ordinary people who have behaved and are behaving with extraordinary heroism and courage in the face of devastation and death. Such stories break open our hearts and fill us with hope. They are an antidote to the poison of fear.

The seasonal stories we are telling the children are also filled with vibrant images of courage and resolve to protect the good and stand guard over truth, whatever the cost. These stories reassure the children that there are many human beings who, through their own volition and inner certainty of a "guiding presence," have faced the dragon and prevailed. Such beings are the Protectors. We must let the children know that these Protectors are among us, invisibly living in strangers, neighbors, friends and even in our own hearts.

Let us strive now to become Protectors, and may each story, old and new, awaken us to what is true and highest and most worthy of protection!

My second graders performed in a Michaelmas play as townspeople who, led by a brave young girl, were able to defeat and eventually tame a fierce dragon. When they were in seventh grade, they got to be the dragon. The following is an excerpt from a parent letter I wrote home the following Sunday:

> Those of you who were not able to come to the Michaelmas assembly missed an extraordinary feat on the part of the seventh-grade dragon, which, forgive me, looked a bit more like a deranged centipede. The feat, second only to St. George's slaying and resurrection, was that all the dragon's feet (48?) moved together to a short-short-long drumbeat and none of them got tangled up, bringing the dragon down before its time.
>
> Our class is a very strong group, and the dragon was the ultimate test of their ability to work together and fall in line when necessary. Impressive, particularly because we only had two short practices.

After Michaelmas and the Harvest Fair, a community picnic with games and concessions, food and music, and handcrafts for sale, the children began to plan for Hallowe'en, my least favorite school celebration. I did not mind the actual day with costumes and festivities, but the week leading up to it has to be the most difficult teaching challenge of the year, filled as it is with ghosts, sprites, and goblins of various sorts. Fortunately, at our school, we also celebrated the Day of the Dead on November 2, which helped the children settle back into themselves and deepen their understanding of the holiday.

Our handwork teacher, Adele Maze, had been collecting *Día de los Muertos* figures, cutouts and decorations for many years. The children in each class brought framed pictures of loved ones who had died — grandparents, siblings, friends, dogs, cats, and rabbits. These pictures were interspersed with the colorful offerings, flowers, and figures on tables in an empty classroom. One class at a time silently entered the darkened room and sat on the floor in front of the *ofrenda* for about fifteen minutes, listening to music — sometimes a guitar, sometimes a cello—and looking at the pictures flickering in the candle flames. The children were reverent. There was never any pushing or poking, and I remember being touched to see tears streaming down the face of one of my liveliest first-grade boys. When the children left the room, they were given hot chocolate and a bun to eat together in the classroom. The discussion that ensued was always thoughtful and quiet as the children told stories about their loved pets or family members who had died.

Celebrations continued throughout the dark of the year. The fifth graders celebrated Divali, the Indian Feast of Light, while the second graders chose a Santa Lucia, who, with her attendants, brought light and special treats to each classroom. Advent and Chanukah candles were lit in each classroom in the mornings, honoring the mineral, plant, animal, and human kingdoms, and the third graders recounted Hebrew stories of courage under great duress. Secret friends exchanged little gifts during the week before the Christmas holidays, and St. Nicholas, with his sidekick Rupert, visited classes to see who had been naughty or nice. On the last day of school before Christmas break, the faculty performed one of the medieval mystery plays, *The Shepherds Play*, and the children took delight in discovering which part their teacher would play.

Spring was filled with game days, often involving other schools: the Pentathlon (featuring wrestling, racing, discus, and javelin) for fifth-grade students of ancient Greece, the Medieval Games for sixth grade (featuring archery, jousting, and tug of war), and track meets for the seventh and eighth grades. We celebrated spring at the May Faire by crowning a seventh-grade king and queen, making and wearing flower wreaths and spending the afternoon dancing around the maypole, playing music and feasting. Interspersed with these seasonal events were a number of concerts, all school assemblies and class plays performed by the children for the whole school community.

Every year, an exhausted teacher or parent (or two) would propose cutting back the event schedule, and every year, no one could agree on what to cut. It was all valuable, important, and worth doing, connecting us, adults and children, to the earth, the seasons, our human past, and each other. We all had to learn how to simply enjoy the moment. We could either see these events as burdensome tasks or as opportunities to lightly and joyfully express our appreciation to each other and the great forces of nature that support our mutual life.

Eighth grade had a poignant sensibility as my now young adolescents participated in each celebration for the last time. Students prepared and presented their eighth-grade projects, performed *The Skin of Our Teeth*, went on a week-long trip to Catalina Island and Santa Barbara, and then prepared for our final day together: our eighth-grade graduation. The children wrote a humorous and touching script, starting with their mutual memories of kindergarten and the grades. I noted that not one of their memories recalled the content of their academic lessons.

On our last day on Catalina, our guides planned a hike to the top of the island. The afternoon was hot, and I discovered about two-thirds of the way to the summit that my pulse was beginning to race. Collapsing from heat stroke was not a good prospect, so I found a tree with a little shade and told the climbers that I would sit under it, think about my graduation speech, and join them on the way down. There was some concern among the students because it was the first time that I had been unable to rise to a challenge, literally in this case. I told them it would be fine and they would soon be going on without me all the time. I pondered my speech, wrote down my thoughts and drank all my water. After a few hours, we reunited, and it was all downhill from there.

A few days later, in Santa Barbara, before we boarded the train back to Northern California, we gathered in a circle, and student after student let me know that they already knew everything I planned to say to them. I was even more anxious when I heard their graduation speeches a few days later. What remained for me to say to them, particularly in front of all the parents and colleagues? I decided to speak from my heart. I recounted some of my thoughts, how my students had already expressed them much better than

I could, and how gratifying that was. My job was done, and they were all demonstrating that they were ready for the next step in their journeys. It was time for us to celebrate together and express our gratitude for the circle of the school, the circle of parents, and the spirit of this group of children. Then I shared with them a poem that I had written the night before:

BECAUSE OF YOU
Because of you
the holes in my childhood are gone.
They filled as we played our circle games
and told fairy tales,
as we held hands while leaving the garden
and helped each other find our way
in the wide world of myth and history.
Because of you
fifty-two years between our births
dissolve when I see in you
something that was silent in myself
until you came and woke it up
so I could share it with you.
Because of you
I recently pretended to be a truffala tree
and skipped down a path with two barbaloos
until I tripped and we fell in a heap laughing.
People stared.
Has Mrs. Cummings lost her mind?
Which mind?
I will be less opinionated and more adventuresome,
less fearful and more free spirited,
less serious and more young at heart,
because of you.
You are my hope for the future,
not because you are individually better than other people,
not only because of what you will do later,

but because of what you already are together,
loving life, learning to give and receive, being vulnerable
and feeling gratitude to each other.
Like I do
because of you.

HOW TO CELEBRATE THE RICHNESS
OF OUR MULTICULTURAL WORLD WITHOUT
VIOLATING THE SEPARATION OF CHURCH AND STATE

1. **Explore opportunities for celebrative events in your school community.** Waldorf public charter schools operate within the general guidelines for public education and adapt their celebrative practices to honor the principles of separation of church and state. Seasonal festivals such as a Harvest Fair or May Faire are not based on any current religious practice and can be community celebrations. Hallowe'en and Day of the Dead are more controversial. Although they were originally pagan festivals, they were absorbed by the Catholic Church before they became more generalized by the culture. Wearing a costume for Hallowe'en is not a religious observance.

   Students in a public school can learn about the Day of the Dead, but parents should be informed if a class or school decides to have an *ofrenda*. This is, however, a powerful celebration for children who are dealing with death in the family or the death of pets, and it can be done simply as a cultural festival without religious overtones.

   Gift sharing with a little food before the winter break can also be done in a non-religious manner. Our class drew names and brought their secret friend simple gifts during the week preceding our winter break—a cookie, a drawing, a piece of candy. Another option is a white elephant party where students can share toys and books.

   Inform parents when planning events. Parents should know what to expect and be given the opportunity to express concerns.

2. **Invite parents to talk about their cultural and religious backgrounds with the children through stories and or treats on special days.**

3. **Allow children in multicultural classrooms to teach each other about celebrations that are part of their ethnic or religious communities.** There is no legal prescription against talking about religion. It is advised, however, to come to an understanding with administration and with parents, explaining why such discussions are essential to an informed citizenry in a multicultural democracy.

4. **Take up the question of seasonal celebrations with your faculty circle as part of planning for each school year.** Engage parents in planning and implementation and allow for open discussion and questions.

For Parents: Build community by participating in all seasonal celebrations. These events depend on parents for planning and execution as well as attendance. Celebrations offer the children experiences of a larger community that supports and nurtures their growth.

Each class community participates as part of a larger community of the school, giving children a direct experience of what to expect in the future.

. . . . .

Rudolf Steiner told his teachers that they could measure their success by the amount of life force and enthusiasm present in their students. This enthusiasm is precious, and it is contagious; it tells us the doors to learning are open and we are energized to act, to create, to begin to make new connections. Steiner warned that if we educate children to be adjusted to the expectations of the world as it is, we will paralyze their potential. He charged his teachers to nurture each child by helping them realize their special gifts and abilities.

We spent many hours a week working on the curriculum—on history, math, literature, science, and the arts. Learning happened best when students (of all ages) were intrinsically involved in the process and encouraged to articulate and follow their own questions and come to their own conclusions. The more I attended to their questions, the more my students were able to shape me to their needs. This ongoing exchange was key to our success as a group of learners.

My students inspired me to take risks, to create activities, stories, or experiences in response to what I saw in them. Their responding contributions and creations filled me with joy. This collaboration and the energized community that developed as we learned together gave us wings.

My students were well prepared academically and would later avidly pursue their intellectual and artistic interests through high school and college. But their first eight years of school were focused primarily on building a strong physical and emotional platform for later intellectual and artistic development, a platform built through stories, play, strenuous physical activity, creative expression, strong relationships, and community support.

The academic skills we developed, the math and algebra problems we solved, the history we researched, and the many activities we participated in were compost for deeper and more essential capacities of mind and spirit.

Their connection and sense of responsibility to the world around them also expanded as they became more self-aware, self-confident, and socially cohesive as young adolescents. This growth cannot be assessed by multiple-choice tests, but it shines out from the following poems, collected as *Poems for Peace* during a project led by the students' handwork teacher, Adele Maze, in the spring of their seventh-grade year.

> *PUT INTO WORDS*
> *I can hear my thoughts*
> *they're in and out of my head faster than I can write them*

no rhythm
meaningless
until put into words
with jerky background music
a song I only know part of
over and over comes again and again
urging my thoughts
telling me to sing a song
I do not wish to sing
The words are not mine
I do not agree
I can still hear my thoughts
over the noise
they're telling me to
sing out
to write my OWN song.

– Linnea

ON A ROLL
I can roll
where I want to go
a freedom
of choice
a voice
out of a million
I can decide
what I am going to do
to dream of a world anew
I have desire
to transform
will power
to work
I can roll
where I want to go.

– Kaleb

SCENTED WITH ROSES
I came to be woven
into a being of light
and of darkness woven
into light.
Woven strands of light
bent to the colors of the earth
scented with roses
and wrapped around a queen,
a queen with a dream,
a dream to change the world
a world of peace.

— **Theron**

THE GLISTENING WEB
It depends
on what you call "understanding"
the fragile earth
a perfect balance
the tiny mosquito is caught
in the glistening webs of the long-legged spider
who disappears
into the blue jay's beak
the blue jay's life is overcome
a flower grows
from the earth where he lays
a bumblebee alights
gathers nectar for the hive
a bear reaches in a paw
and licks golden honey
It depends
on what you call "understanding"
the fragile earth
a perfect balance.

— **Gwen**

CHECK ME OUT
I open for others.
I share, entertain, and teach.
My contents and knowledge
Exist to wait
and show others my wisdom.
Read.
Learn.
No book should get dusty.

— Jasper

MY PAINTING
I want to be useful
someone people can not ignore.
I want to gather the scattered pieces of our culture
and restore the shattered puzzle's picture.
I want to resolve the world's problems,
to finish my painting of peace.

— Clayton

OUT OF ORDER
Life is out of order
I act without thinking
unaware of the terrible consequences.
Life is out of order
I take without giving
unaware of the despair I am causing.
Nature is in chaos
I'll restore harmony.
I stand out of line
I'll get back in my place.
Our world is broken.
I'll fix it.

— Joey

These young voices tell us that their natural capacities for learning are maturing. They tell us in voices that are becoming distinctly individual about their shared commitment to making a difference in a world in grave need of transformation. They are becoming members of a community committed to the ongoing transformation of both self and society.

My experience with these students can best be described as a labor of love that gave birth to capacities of mind and spirit. A love-based education that respects the natural ways that children learn supported us to become resilient, lifelong learners who respond to challenges by overcoming fear and growing in our capacity to create and collaborate. I am grateful for the opportunity to experience that such an education is possible. I want every child and teacher on this planet to have that opportunity.

Epilogue

John Holt and Rudolf Steiner inspired and supported my growth as a teacher. Their influence led to my appreciation of the natural ways that children learn as I taught through the grades in Waldorf schools. Two recent books, *The Dawn of Everything: A New History of Humanity* by David Wengrow and David Graeber and *Sustainability, Human Well-Being and the Future of Education,* a project of Sitra, the Finnish Innovation Fund, suggest strong support for natural learning and transformation of the content, structure, and methods of our current educational system. *The Dawn of Everything* challenges the assumptions underlying our understanding of the history of civilization and the resulting myths that are referenced to support hierarchical systems of power and control. The authors wonder:

> *What if we treat people from the beginning as imaginative, intelligent, playful creatures who deserve to be understood as such? What if, instead of telling a story about how our species fell from some idyllic state of equality, we ask how we came to be trapped in such tight conceptual shackles that we can no longer even imagine the possibility of reinventing ourselves?*[88]

In *Sustainability, Human Well-Being and the Future of Education,* educators from Finland and the United States respond collaboratively to a similar urgent question: how must our established education system be repurposed and transformed to create the kind of society capable of meeting the exponential environmental and social challenges that are facing the twenty-first-century world?

Graeber and Wengrow review the archeological and anthropological evidence of recent decades and bring to light a complex, nuanced view of human history from the Paleolithic to the present that upends the myth of human progress through distinct developmental stages. They review what we know about early cultures on all continents, including cities with large populations, that were primarily egalitarian and non-hierarchical and moved fluidly through different organizational frameworks depending on the needs of the season. Such societies were based on three primordial freedoms — the freedom to move away, the freedom to disobey, and the freedom to transform social relationships. They provided a schismogenic contrast to oppressive, patriarchal warrior societies in which violent systems of control were normalized.

Access to this book would have profoundly changed the content of high school courses that I taught, from ancient history to the study of ancient Greece and Rome, as well as lower school main lessons in California and U.S. history. How exciting it would have been to teach the children about how the Iroquois and Wendat societies of the Eastern Woodlands and the indigenous tribes of California embraced fundamental freedoms and self-consciously cultivated practices and institutions that offered safety and mutual support to all members without sacrificing agency. What was life like when wealth was shared or gifted rather than amassed for power? I would have told them the story of Kandiaronk, the Wendat philosopher and statesman, who saw society as a confederation based on agreements open to renegotiation. He considered the Europeans he encountered to be pre-logical and primitive, incapable of constructive conversation. Kandiaronk's ideas and critique sparked wide discussion in Europe and resulted in an essay by Rousseau that reputedly sparked the American and French Revolutions. The United States Constitution, in turn, was strongly influenced by Native American standards of republican self-governance.

Wengrow and Graeber challenge the assumption that agricultural practices inevitably triggered top-down hierarchies of governance necessary to support the growth of population and development of civilized society. They describe top-down patriarchal systems that rose and fell throughout our past and were, in many cases, not connected to agricultural practices. Modern states now hold the power once held by pharaohs and kings, buttressed by sophisticated administrative techniques for controlling information and running the economy, a system that is currently breaking down and causing widespread frustration and suffering. Wengrow and Graeber tell us that we can still examine the facts and change the story. They ask what has been lost in the process of the last two thousand years and wonder if we will be able to reclaim our creativity and love of freedom in time. Robert Kelley, Gary Nash endowed chair in U.S. history at UCLA, writes on the back cover of the book:

> *The* Dawn of Everything *introduces us to a world populated by smart, creative, complicated people who, for thousands of years, invent virtually every form of social organization imaginable and pursued freedom, knowledge, experimentation, and happiness way before the Enlightenment.*

Although Wengrow and Graeber do not focus on the education of children through history, their primary message about our human past assumes that children in past egalitarian societies learned naturally by participating fully in civic life, not by sitting quietly in large rooms in front of teachers charged to tell them what they are told they need to know.

Although the eighteen Finnish and American contributors to Sitra's education project come from different perspectives, they fundamentally agree that humanity must find ways to live sustainably within the systems that support planetary life. They also agree that economic structures need to be transformed to foster the well-being of all people without relying on increased consumption of natural resources. Justin Cook, editor and contributor, calls for "learning at the edge of history" in schools that are designed to develop the capacities and competencies that children will need to be capable of bringing this new world into being. To accomplish this unprecedented challenge, they (and we) must question all fundamental assumptions, including how knowledge is organized.

The authors agree that our dated age-based system that divides students into "tracks" and knowledge into "subjects" that are transmitted and tested by teachers is failing to meet the needs of twenty-first-century children. Suggestions for system change weave throughout the presentations, and the following vision emerges.

Curricular change must involve moving away from siloed subjects to systemic learning that explores and strengthens understanding of the connections between humans, nature, culture, and economy. Schools need to be restructured as cross-generational collaborative communities of inquiry and action in which young people's experiences and concerns will be the primary texts, driving transdisciplinary study and real-world engagement.

In addition to developing new skills, students will learn that they are capable of making a difference. These living/learning communities will be committed to the ongoing transformation of self, school, and the dominant systems of society. Students will become global citizens who, as lifelong learners, are capable of creating and maintaining a sustainable, resilient, socially just world that values the well-being of all humans.

More specifically:

- Students must develop new competencies that can operate in a complex, interconnected world where information is ubiquitous and at our fingertips and change is a constant (Cook and Riordan).

- Students must learn to evaluate and order the constant flow of available information in the digital world and be capable of detecting and managing online risks (Kyllonnen).

- In addition to referencing authority and developing reason, learning must involve hands-on experience and noetic knowing, developing and fostering respect for intuition and creative processes (Fidell).

- Schools must support processes that develop children's latent capacities for empathy and self-reflection. Both capacities promote lives of engagement, transformative action, and responsibility for both the self and the world (Glasser).

- Students must become emotionally literate, able to constructively face and frame painful emotions such as grief, anger, and fear so these emotions motivate rather than disable positive action (Lehtonen et al.).

- Schools must utilize artistic activities that support collaboration, communication, constructive critiquing, and resilience in addition to developing creativity (Nathan).

- Schools must promote lifelong learning for all students with a story of "us" that respects the different experiences, gifts, and talents that live in diverse communities (Kyllonen).

Sitra acknowledges that humanity faces multiple wicked problems, not easily solved. Transforming our educational system is a daunting task, somewhat like picking ourselves up by our bootstraps, given that we are all products of the current system and have been conditioned by it.

Our current schools are profoundly influenced by and implicated in a faltering global economic system that has produced unprecedented growth in material prosperity while corrupting political systems, severely damaging the environment, and intensifying social and economic inequality.

Climate scientists sound urgent warnings that we must act now to transform our fossil-fuel-driven economy to an economy based on renewable energy or face increasingly catastrophic changes to our climate. Large groups of people around the planet are protesting in the streets and squares, demanding greater social equity. Authoritarian governments are on the rise, propping up neoliberal capitalism while threatening democracy and future life on our planet. Even the children, led by Swedish teenager Greta Thunberg, are beginning to strike. They beg us to stop talking about it and do something.

Finding the personal and political will to make the necessary changes to our habits, norms, and expectations presents perhaps the steepest challenge of all, given the way that we have been educated and the stories we have been taught to believe. Sitra is calling on educators to create new stories that will give our children and young people shared direction and purpose, the knowledge that they are capable of making necessary changes, and the skills that will make this transformation a reality.

The hopeful news is that many Finnish schools and some schools in the United States are already firmly on the path to realizing this goal. The even better news is that we don't have to change children; we have to change the way we look at them, trusting that they have priceless gifts and natural abilities that will emerge as we work collaboratively to transform our schools from rigid institutions into works in progress. I can't imagine a more challenging and meaningful mission.

Helpful Resources

RECOMMENDED WEBSITES:

anatbanielmethod.com – For children with noticeable neurological delays, Anat Baniel Method may be heaven sent. Her book demonstrates how even severe brain damage can be ameliorated through physical movement.

bal-a-vis-x.com – I learned about this excellent program from a teacher I was mentoring who had many children with developmental challenges in her first-grade class. This is an excellent program with at least three hundred exercises that can be performed individually with students or with an entire class.

brainbalancecenters.com – Dr. Melillo has established learning centers that help parents and teachers diagnose and treat attention and focus problems without drugs.

braingym.org – Brain Gym offers movement exercises for children to enhance learning and help with developmental delays. Teachers can take workshops to learn the exercises and also view them through videos. I took a workshop and also referred several students to a skilled Brain Gym practitioner with good results.

dianeravitch.com/what-you-can-do? – How to opt out and join the movement against high-stakes testing.

earthschool.org – Sonoma Earth School is a mixed-age outdoor learning environment that connects children with the natural world and with each other. Academics integrated into the context of human relationship and nature create the foundation for deep, lifelong learning that serves the unique identity of each student.

edutopia.org/blog/5-benefits-of-outdoor-education-michael-becker – This article gives detailed information on how to establish an outdoor school experience for sixth graders.

farmtoschool.org – National School Garden Network.

fix.com – How to start a school garden.

habitsofmind.org/institute-for-habits-of-mind – This website was established by Dr. Art Costa and Bena Kallick, directed by James Anderson, with a mission to create a more thoughtful, cooperative, and compassionate generation of people able to resolve social, environmental, economic, and political problems.

hightechhigh.org – A system of equitable public charter schools in San Diego based on student-initiated inquiry.

inquiryinstitute.com – Marilee Adams established this website to promote more consciousness and choice by helping people identify whether they are using "judger mind" or "learner mind." This approach can be adapted to children of any age and is a support to any learning process.

janehealy.com – Dr. Healy helps teachers and parents identify, understand, and treat learning problems.

lindamoodbell.com – Lindamood-Bell Learning Processes is an effective program for children with dyslexia. The program is expensive. I worked with a support teacher who had taken this training at her own expense. A good use of school funds would be to pay for such training for teachers or learning specialists.

marionbrady.com – Marion and Scott Brady on systems-based learning.

mathsolutions.com – Math Solutions is the lifework of mathematics educator Marilyn Burns. Her website is a treasure trove of ideas, challenging lessons, and wisdom. I thank Marilyn and her cohorts for offering me the tools to become a successful math teacher.

neufeldinstitute.org – This website offers courses and presentations for therapists, parents, and teachers based on Dr. Neufeld's attachment-based developmental approach to making sense of children's behavior and establishing strong attachment relationships.

rudolfsteinerpress.com – Publishes books by Rudolf Steiner as well as many books about Waldorf education and anthroposophy.

waldorfeducation.org – Offers general information about Waldorf education

youandyourchildshealth.org – Dr. Susan Johnson is a medical doctor whose quest to help her developmentally challenged son led to a journey of discovery and assistance for parents. An excellent resource.

RECOMMENDED BOOKS:

Adams, Marilee. Teaching *That Changes Lives: 12 Mindset Tools For Igniting a Love of Learning.* San Francisco: Barrett Koehler, 2013.

Ayers, Bill. *Demand the Impossible! A Radical Manifesto.* (Chicago: Haymarket, 2016).

Brown, Robyn. *A Practical Guide to Curative Education: The Ladder of the Seven Life Processes.* Lindisfarne Books, 2016.

Cook, Justin, ed. *Sustainability, Human Well-Being, and the Future of Education.* London: Palgrave McMillan, 2019.

Costa, Arthur L., and Bena Kallich. *Learning and Leading with Habits of Mind: 16 Essential Characteristics for Success.* Association for Supervision and Curriculum Development, 2008.

Elkind, David. *The Power of Play: Learning What Comes Naturally.* Boston: Da Capo, 2017.

Graeber, David, and David Wengrow. *The Dawn of Everything: A New History of Humanity.* New York: Farrar, Strauss and Giroux, 2021.

Given, Barbara K. *Teaching to the Brain's Natural Learning Systems.* Association for Supervision and Curriculum Development, 2002.

Haskell, David G. *The Forest Unseen: A Year's Watch in Nature.* London: Penguin Group, 2012.

Hart, Sura, and Victoria Kindle Hodson, *The Compassionate Classroom: Relationship-Based Teaching and Learning.* Encinitas, CA: PuddleDancer Press, 2004.

Healy, Jane M. *Your Child's Growing Mind: A Practical Guide to Brain Development and Learning from Birth to Adolescence.* New York: Doubleday, 1994.

— — —. *Different Learners: Identifying, Preventing and Treating Your Child's Learning Problems.* New York: Simon and Schuster, 2010.

— — —. *Endangered Minds: Why Children Don't Think and What We Can Do About It.* New York: Touchstone, 1990.

Holt, John. *How Children Learn.* 2nd ed. New York: Perseus Books, 1983.

Maté, Gabor. *Scattered: How Attention Deficit Disorder Originates and What You Can Do About It.* London: Penguin, 2000.

— — —, and Daniel Maté. *The Myth of Normal: Trauma, Illness and Healing in a Toxic Culture.* New York: Avery, 2022.

Mathews, Paul. *Sing Me the Creation.* New York: Hawthorn Press, 1994.

Neufeld, Gordon, and Gabor Maté. *Hold on to Your Kids.* New York: Ballantine Books, 2005.

Olson, Kirsten. *Wounded by School: Recapturing the Joy in Learning and Standing Up to Old School Culture.* New York: Teacher's College Press, 2009.

Pearce, Joseph C. *Magical Child.* New York: Dutton, 1977.

Riley, Phillip. *Attachment Theory and the Teacher-Student Relationship.* Milton Park, Abingdon, Oxfordshire: Routledge, 2010.

Robinson, Ken, and Lou Aronica. *Creative Schools: The Grassroots Revolution That's Transforming Education.* New York: Viking, 2015.

Rosenberg, Marshall B. *Life-Enriching Education: Nonviolent Communication Helps Schools Improve Performance, Reduce Conflict, and Enhance Relationships.* Encinitas, CA: PuddleDancer Press, 2003.

Smyth, Nell. *Drama at the Heart: Teaching Drama in Steiner-Waldorf Schools.* Edinburgh: Floris Books, 2016.

Spaulding, Romalda B. *The Writing Road to Reading.* 6th rev. ed. Spaulding Education International, 1957.

Acknowledgments

I acknowledge my students, who taught me through direct experience most of what I know about how children learn. I particularly thank the Marin Waldorf School Class of 2006, who traveled eight years with me through the grades, keeping me on my toes every day. My experiences with you form the living heart of this book through your stories, poems, and words. Particular thanks to Hannah Liberman, Max Perry, Josef Mehling, Lily Weber-Gil, and Kaleb Ganz for adding their reflections and memories to my manuscript. Special thanks to Michael Ostling, a brilliant former student at Summerfield Waldorf School in Santa Rosa, California.

Deep gratitude to my colleagues over many years who shared their ideas, creative talents, and knowledge while we learned together how to work collaboratively and consensually. Karen Rivers, thank you for helping me get started on a new path. Justin Ganz, I thank you for giving so generously of your time and providing a balance to my efforts with your inspiring physical games and activities. Kalen Wood, your friendship, colleagueship, and encouragement have been a steady blessing.

I couldn't have accomplished what I did without the parents who created a village of support and love around their children by coming to our meetings and events, driving on trips, and making our celebrations possible. Special thanks to Eileen Leatherman, whose quiet, steady organizational support enabled many of our trips, adventures, and events, and to Gary Malkin, whose extraordinary musical talent enhanced our plays and performances. Special recognition to Charissa Drengsen, Marien Grace, and Robert and Leslie Currier, who wrote plays, designed and constructed sets, and collected costumes to support our theatrical productions through the years.

I thank Michael Becker at Hood River Junior High in Hood River, Oregon, for allowing me to visit his classes and interview his students so I could see project-based learning in action. Special appreciation to Aiden Cross, Joe Reitz, Cole Duckwall, and Emma Kelly for their perspectives.

Special thanks to Gordon Neufeld, Frances Weller, Marion Brady, Art Costa, Bill Ayres, Bill McKibben, Marya Hornbacher, Reggie Melrose, and Betty Staley, who have encouraged me with their examples and kind assessments.

Gratitude to Nora Profit, director of The Writing Loft, for her guidance as I transformed *What Are We Going To Learn Today* into *Trust Children* and to Ruth Schwartz, the Wonderlady, and her team who helped me publish my book. Special thanks to Jefferson from FirstEditing for his expert formatting and proofreading and Lorna Johnson for an awesome cover design and interior layout.

Finally, I thank my family: my brother and sister, David and Linda Haskell and my late husband, Roland Jacopetti, for their unconditional support and willingness to read drafts and comment on them, Kiki La Porta, who has shared her considerable design talents, my son Kelsey, whose computer skills have averted catastrophe, and my daughters-in-law, Emily Stock and Stacey Cummings, for their diligence as proofreaders.

About the Author

Anne Cummings Jacopetti grew up in a family of educators, graduated Phi Beta Kappa in Dramatic Art and English at UC Berkeley and completed a MA in Theater Arts at the University of Minnesota.

She was accepted into U.C.'s Graduate Internship Program, which offered a direct path into teaching for a select group of college graduates and professionals. This program sparked collaborations, grant applications and projects, including the first "school-within-a-school" pilot program, as well as projects designed to integrate diverse groups of students. The projects at Friend's Select School in Philadelphia and at Berkeley High in California are described in Terry Borton's *Reach, Touch and Teach* (McGraw Hill, 1970).

For the next twenty years she taught high school and junior college, supervised teachers through the Graduate Internship Program and led workshops and classes for teachers at UC, UCSC, the State Arts Commission, and the Teachers Active Learning Center in San Francisco. She was on the staff of Upward Bound at Sonoma State University and participated in an Upward Bound program at Western Reserve Academy in Ohio.

After being introduced to Waldorf education by friend and mentor, M.C. Richards, Anne accepted a position at Marin Waldorf

School as a fourth-grade teacher and began to study Waldorf education at Rudolf Steiner College in Fair Oaks, California. She subsequently helped to pioneer a high school at Summerfield Waldorf School in Santa Rosa. In 1998 she returned to MWS and met the group of first graders she would lead for the next eight years. The Class of 2006 was the largest graduating class in the school's history.

After retiring from teaching, Anne supervised beginning Waldorf teachers for Touro University and Rudolf Steiner College and was hired as School Mentor at Live Oak Public Charter School in Petaluma, California. Her final three years before full retirement were spent as Education Director at Woodland Star Charter School in Sonoma, California.

***Children learn best
the ways they've always learned...***

through building community

through stories

through practicing the arts

through questioning

through direct experience

through reconnecting with nature

through celebrating

through play

through overcoming challenges

through relationship

Endnotes

1   en.wikipedia.org/wiki/Waldorf_education#Origins_and_history.

2   Beth Skwarecki, "Babies Learn to Recognize Words in the Womb," *sciencemag.org/news/2013/08/babies-learn-recognize-words-womb.*

3   Norman Doidge, *The Brain that Changes Itself* (London: Penguin Group, 2007).

4   Barbara K. Given, *Teaching to the Brains' Natural Learning Systems* (Association for Supervision and Curriculum Development, 2002), vii.

5   Ibid., 136.

6   https://www.brookings.edu/blog/education-plus-development/ 2019/02/14/integrating-21st-century-skills-into-education-systems-from-rhetoric-to-reality/.

7   https://www.pblglobal.com/empathy-holds-key-transforming-21st-century-learning.

8   Ken Robinson and Lou Aronica, *Creative Schools: The Grassroots Revolution That's Transforming Education* (London: Penguin Books, 2015).

9   Justin Cook, ed., *Sustainability, Human Well Being and the Future of Education,* https://www.springer.com/us/book/9783319785790? wt_mc=ThirdParty.SpringerLink.3.EPR653.About_eBook# otherversion=9783319785806.

10 Bill Ayers, *Demand the Impossible! A Radical Manifesto* (Chicago: Haymarket Books, 2016), 161.

11 John Holt, *How Children Fail* (Boston: Pitman Publishing, 1964), 208.

12 Holt, *How Children Learn*, rev. ed., (New York: Perseus Books, 1983), 287.

13 John Howard Griffin, *Black Like Me* (New York: Houghton Mifflin, 1961).

14 Viola Spolin, *Improvisation for the Theatre: A Handbook of Teaching and Directing Techniques* (Evanston, IL: Northwestern University Press, 1963).

15 Terry Borton, *Reach, Touch and Teach: Student Concerns and Process Education* (New York: McGraw Hill, 1970), 190.

16 Holt, *How Children Learn*, 13.

17 Audrey L. Amrein and David C. Berliner, *"The Effect of High Stakes Testing on Student Motivation and Learning,"* https://wou.edu/~girodm/611/testing_and_motivation.pdf.

18 Mary Caroline Richards, *Towards Wholeness: Rudolf Steiner Education in America* (Middletown, CTL Wesleyan University Press, 1980).

19 Peter Selg, *The Essence of Waldorf Education* (New York: Steiner Books, 2010) 22–27.

20 http.//www.psychologistworld.com/developmental/attachment-theory.

21 Gordon Neufeld and Gabor Maté, *Hold on to Your Kids* (New York: Ballantine, 2005), 213.

22 https://www.psychologytoday.com/us/blog/call/201703/when-childhood-trauma-meets-healing-relationships.

23 https://www.ctsatherapy.com/healing-childhood-trauma-through-relationship/.

24 Otto Scharmer, *Essentials of Theory U: Core Principles and Applications* (Oakland, CA: Berrett-Koehler, 2018), 24.

25 Peter Steig, *The Essence of Waldorf Education* (Spencertown, NY: Steiner Books, 2010), 30.

26 http://www.anatbanielmethod.com.

27 Phillip Riley, *Attachment Theory and the Teacher-Student Relationship: A Practical Guide for Teachers, Teacher Educators and School Leaders* (Milton Park, Abingdon, Oxfordshire: Routledge, 2010).

28 www.neufeldinstitute.org.

29 https://www.waldorfpublications.org/blogs/book-news/being-nine-years-old.

30 https://www.ericdigests.org/20024/schools.html.

31 www.inquiryinstitute.com.

32 Colin Wells, "From Memory to Innovation: The Vowel Revolution in the Making of the Modern Mind," *The Hedgehog Review,* Fall 2018, 111.

33 The following quote is from an article by Dr. Susan Johnson, "A Developmental Approach Looking at the Relationship of Children's' Foundational Neurological Pathways to Their Higher Capacities for Learning":

> *In our world today, children are often labeled with disorders like ADHD, various learning challenges and anxiety. My clinical experience, from more than 30 years of evaluating children, has taught me that most of these labels occur when we teach children to write, read, spell, and do written math too early, before they are neurologically ready. In addition, some children need more time for their neurological, learning pathways to fully develop, especially if they received excessive force on their craniums during the birth process (i.e. cranial compressions), are exceptionally bright, and/or have increased artistic and intuitive capacities.*
>
> *In these instances, the right side of a child's brain would need a longer time to develop or myelinate, before they would be ready to use the left parietal area of their brain to sound-out words phonetically. In general, girls may not be ready to start to phonetically read until ages 6 1/2 to 8 years of age, while boys may not be ready to start to phonetically read until ages 7 1/2 to 9 years of age, and sometimes later for both boys and girls (because of the reasons already noted). Sight (i.e. spatial) reading, which occurs in the right side of the brain, can be used to recognize the shape of words as early as ages 3 1/2 or 4 years of age and sometimes even earlier. Yet, this same right area of the brain has a much more important task, which is to create inner-imaginative pictures and scenes related to the words that the child is reading or even listening to. http://youandyourchildshealth.org/articles/teaching-our-children.html.*

34 https://us.humankinetics.com/blogs/excerpt/how-physical-activity-and-exercise-enhance-childrens-cognition.

35 Jane M. Healy, *Your Child's Growing Mind: A Practical Guide to Brain Development and Learning from Birth to Adolescence* (New York: Doubleday, 1994), 63.

36 https://edpolicy.stanford.edu/sites/default/files/publications/scope-report-waldorf-inspired-school.pdf, 98.

37 Romalda B. Spaulding, *Writing Road to Reading*, 6th ed. (New York: Harper Collins, 2012).

38 Rebecca Solnit, *The Faraway Nearby* (London: Penguin Books, 2014), 3.

39 https://www.researchgate.net/publication/234763056_Memory_Imagination_and_Lear ning_Connected_by_the_Story.

40 Ibid.

41 https://waldorfish.com/blog/pedagogical-stories-start.

42 https.//www.cjr.org/covering_climate_now.

43 Stuart Brown, *Play: How It Shapes the Brain, Opens the Imagination, and Invigorates the Soul* (New York: Penguin Books, 2009), 32.

44 Ibid., 33–34.

45 Ibid., 36

46 Paul Mathews, *Sing Me the Creation* (New York: Hawthorn Press, 1994).

47 http://www.npr.org/sections/ed/2016/01/03/460254858/turns-out=monkey-bars-and-kickball-are-good-for-the-brain.

48 https://www.huffpost.com/entry/attention-deficit-disorde_b_541581

49 https://www.cdc.gov/ncddd/adhd/features/keyfindings-adhd72013.html.

50 http://www.sph.sc.edu?news/mckeown6.html.

51 https://www.psychologytoday.com/blog/suffer-the-children/201203/why-french-kids-dont-have-adhd.

52 http://www.nytimew.com/2013/12/19/opinion/an-epidemic-of-attention-deficit-disorder.html.

53 http:///drgabormaté.com/article/how-not-to-deal-with-hyperactivity.

54 Ibid., 60–62.

55 http://www.truthdig.com/report/item/how_to_think_20120709.

56 http://www.truthdig.com/report/item/how_to_think_20120709.

57 https://www.youtube.com/results?search_query=Copper+wimmin+2016.

58 www.edutopia.org/stw-arts-integration-reform-overview.

59 Ayers *Demand the Impossible,* 164

60 Arthur Costa, *Developing Minds: A Resource Book for Teaching Thinking,* (Alexandria VA: ASCD, 2001), 80.

61 http://inquiryinstitute.com/resources/top-12-questions.

62 http://habitsofmindinstitute.org.

63 http://teachthoughtwegrowteachers.org.

64 http://www.habitsofmindinstitute.org/about-us/hear-art.

65 https://mathsolutions.com.

66 Marion Brady, "The Big Problem with the Common Core That Keeps Getting Ignored," *Washington Post,* October 22, 2015. To access Marion Brady's extensive writings and course materials see http://www.marionbrady.com.

67 https://www.hightechhigh.org/about-us/#.

68 https://link.springer.com/content/pdf/10.1007%2F978-3-319-78580-6.pdf.

69 https://www.hightechhigh.org.

70 https://www.freire.org/paulo-freire.

71 http://www.marionbrady.com.

72 www.bie.org.

73 https://link.springer.com/content/pdf/10.1007%2F978-3-319-78580-6.pdf, 152.

74 https://medlineplus.gov/ency/patientinstructions/000355.htm.

75 http://www.hsph.harvard.edu/obesity-prevention-source/obesity-causes/television-and-sedentarybehavior-and-obesity.

76 https://www.nationwidechildrens.org/newsroom/news-releases/2023/09/adhd-medication-errors-study.

77 Regalena "Reggie" Melrose, "Why Waldorf Works: From a Neuroscientific Perspective," https://blog.waldorfmoraine.org › *2017/07.*

78 Scott Sampson, *How to Raise a Wild Child* (New York: Houghton Mifflin, 2015), 9.

79 http://www.childrenandnature.org.

80 Francis Weller, *The Wild Edge of Sorrow* (Berkeley, CA: North Atlantic Books, 2015), 50.

81 Mary Caroline Richards, *Imagine Inventing Yellow* (New York: Institute for Publishing Arts, 1991) 92.

82 *www.edutopia.org/blog/5-benefits-of-outdoor-education-michael-becker.*

83 https://naturebridge.org.

84 www.parks.ca.gov./?page_id=27635.

85 https://hwos.com/.

86 www.hikethedivide.com.

87 Wendell Berry, *Life is A Miracle: An Essay Against Modern Superstition* (Berkeley, CA: Counterpoint, 2001), 43.

88 David Graeber and David Wengrow, *The Dawn of Everything: A New History of Humanity* (New York: Farrar, Strauss and Giroux, 2021), 9.

Our children are our most precious resource. Protecting and nurturing this resource is an awesome responsibility shared by teachers and parents.

We understand now that our actions and words and the experiences we create literally shape and determine not only the minds and hearts of our children, but also the future of our society.

Will our children be vibrant, creative thinkers and problem solvers, capable of empathy and collaboration as well as individual achievement? Or will our children's innate capacities be stunted, their voices and questions silenced, their contributions frustrated or deterred in an increasingly depleted and repressive world?

Through my blog and my book I hope to share widely what I have learned from children about what they need to thrive and love learning.

I invite you to join this inquiry by sharing your experiences and thoughts. I will post your comments and questions on my blog.

My intention is to spark an essential conversation offering inspiration and encouragement to our dedicated teachers and parents and to the beautiful children that depend on them.

Please visit my website and my blog at:
howchildrenlearn.org

You can scan the QR code to take you directly to the website: